Ronald W. Reagan
40th President of the United States

Neal E. Robbins

 GARRETT EDUCATIONAL CORPORATION

Copyright © 1990 by Neal E. Robbins

Manufactured in the United States of America

Edited and produced by Synthegraphics Corporation

Library of Congress Cataloging in Publication Data

Robbins, Neal E., 1954-
  Ronald W. Reagan, 40th President of the United States / Neal E. Robbins.
      p.   cm. — (Presidents of the United States)
  Includes bibliographical references.
  Summary: Presents the life of Ronald Reagan, including his childhood, education, employment, and political career.
    1. Reagan, Ronald—Juvenile literature.   2. Presidents—United States—Biography—Juvenile literature.   3. United States—Politics and government—1981–1989—Juvenile literature.   [1. Reagan, Ronald.   2. Presidents.]
  I. Title.   II. Series.
E877.R65   1990
973.927'092—dc20
[B]
[92]   89-39955
ISBN 0-944483-66-6   CIP
                                                                    AC

Contents

Chronology for
Ronald W. Reagan

1911   Born on February 6 in Tampico, Illinois

1928– Attended Eureka College
1932

1933– Worked as a radio sports announcer in
1937   Iowa

1937   Began 27-year career as a motion picture
           actor

1940   Married Jane Wyman on January 26

1942– Served in the U.S. Air Force film unit in
1945   Los Angeles

1947– Served five terms as president of Screen
1952   Actors Guild

1948   Divorced from Jane Wyman

1952   Married Nancy Davis on March 4

1954– Hosted dramatic television shows
1965

1959– Served sixth term as president of Screen
1960   Actors Guild

1967– Served two terms as governor of
1975   California

1980   Elected 40th President of the United
           States

1984   Re-elected to second term as President

1989   Retired to Bel-Air, California

Chapter 1

A Town Called Dixon

U nder the brightly shining midday sun, the world's two most powerful leaders took a stroll in Moscow's Red Square. The breeze blew lightly as the younger but balding leader of the Soviet Union, Mikhail Gorbachev, and the neatly groomed President of the United States, Ronald Reagan, calmly moved across the vast plaza in the center of Moscow. On this Tuesday, May 31, 1988, they were taking a break from a summit meeting in the nearby Soviet government headquarters, the Kremlin.

Aides, secret service guards, reporters, and cameramen hovered around as Gorbachev showed his visitor the notched Kremlin walls and onion-domed church bordering the historic square. When a woman walked by, the smiling Gorbachev greeted her and plucked a boy from her arms. As Gorbachev held the boy, he instructed him to "Shake hands with Grandfather Reagan." The President cuddled the boy briefly before the leaders headed back to the Kremlin.

"ANOTHER TIME, ANOTHER ERA"

To millions who glimpsed the tiny scene, even though it was staged, the moment marked a stunning change in world affairs. For decades the Soviet Union and the United States had fought a "cold war," wrangling for the upper hand in every arena of international politics and military prowess. Now, the leaders of these two nations were acting like old friends. Most remarkable was seeing President Reagan, who had criticized the Soviet Union many times in his years in politics, standing in a neat blue suit with a big smile on his face in the heart of Moscow.

A few minutes after the Red Square visit, back inside the Kremlin, a reporter asked Reagan whether he still thought of the Soviet Union as the "evil empire." Early in his presidency, he had once called the Soviet Union that and said the Soviet leaders were capable of any crime. Now, looking a bit uncomfortable, the President shook his head and said, "No, I was talking about another time, another era."

A Warming of Relations

That other "era" was a time, not so long before, when the United States and the Soviet Union looked like sworn enemies and Reagan an uncompromising champion of anti-Communism. But that time had passed. The Soviet Union began to change and, in the last year of his two-term presidency, Reagan ushered in an unprecedented warming of U.S.-Soviet relations. With Gorbachev, he negotiated agreements curbing the arms race and reducing the threat of nuclear war, paving the way for an end to the Cold War. To mark these achievements, the greatest successes of his second term, perhaps of his presidency, Reagan walked shoulder to shoulder with the Soviet leader in Red Square.

That this moment should occur on the world stage seemed fitting, for Reagan had long sought and thrived in the public spotlight. He began his working life as a youthful lifeguard who liked to be seen and heard. Later, as a radio sports announcer, he earned celebrity status for his vivid retellings of baseball games. Then he became a national figure as a friendly faced Hollywood movie and television actor. He then served as the outspoken governor of California before seeking the presidency, where he became one of the shapers of this century.

Yet Ronald Reagan began life simply. He grew up in the heartland of America, in a place much like many others — a town of ordinary people and modest ways.

MOVING ON

On December 6, 1920, the Reagan family was about to pile into the car to move from the dot-on-the-map town of Tampico to a new home in Dixon, 26 miles away over the countryside of northwest Illinois. For a week, Jack Reagan, the father of the family, had been getting the two boys excited about their new home, telling them that Dixon was "a big city" where the circus came and where the new house would have a yard they could play in. The boys couldn't wait to leave.

Everything was ready for going to Dixon, a town of 8,191 people, except for one snag: nine-year-old Ronald's cat Guinevere had just had kittens: Arthur, Sir Galahad, and Buster. With the second-hand automobile already piled high with possessions, Jack wanted to leave the kittens behind, but his wife, Nelle, rescued them. She tucked the animals into a covered basket in the back seat. With everyone loaded into the car and after a picture-taking session with neighbors, they drove away.

Though the Reagans had moved around Illinois many times, this was more than just another move. For a second and last time they were leaving behind Tampico (population 849). The town had been the focus of the family's early life at a time when Jack's ambitions for a better job and his drinking habits had forced the Reagans to migrate from city to city—from Tampico to Chicago, to Galesburg, to Monmouth, and back to Tampico again—living in one rented apartment after another. Jack kept most work briefly because of his addiction to alcohol.

A Religious Mother

Nelle had taken refuge in Christianity. On Easter, March 27, 1910, in Tampico, just before she became pregnant with Ronald, she had converted to the Disciples of Christ, a fundamentalist offshoot of Presbyterianism. The conversion of Nelle, who probably had attended a Methodist church during her girlhood on an Illinois farm, was apparently profound. She became a zealous local missionary, teaching Bible school, distributing religious pamphlets, and putting on morality plays she wrote herself. She visited mental hospitals and prisons to give Bible readings.

At home, Nelle waged a personal war on liquor, praying on her knees several times a day for her hard-drinking Roman Catholic husband. But Jack's thirst for whiskey grew, and religion divided the family.

After Nelle and Jack married on November 8, 1904, in a Catholic church, the couple had made a pact to bring up their children in the Catholic faith until they reached an age when they could choose for themselves. Their first child, John Neil, was baptized as a Catholic. But after Nelle's conversion, she broke the agreement, raising the children in the Disciples church.

"Dutch" and "Moon"

Ronald Wilson Reagan was born on a snowbound February 6, 1911. The blue-eyed, auburn-haired Nelle gave birth in the family's five-room apartment over a general store on Tampico's Main Street. Ronald squealed so loudly on emerging that Jack commented to the attending midwife and doctor, "For such a little bit of a fat Dutchman, he makes a . . . lot of noise, doesn't he?"

"I think he's perfectly wonderful," Nelle said weakly.

Jack later boasted to the townspeople about his robust new child, his "fat little Dutchman," which was how Ronald came to be nicknamed "Dutch."

The arrival of Dutch brought joy; it also fueled tensions in the household. His elder brother, John Neil, born in the same apartment on September 16, 1908, had been sent downstairs to live with neighbors when the baby arrived.

"Now you can go home and see your baby brother," John Neil was told several days later. But for two days, the older boy refused to visit his mother and brother.

"I didn't want any part of my brother," John Neil said later. "I had been promised a sister by my mother and father. That's all I wanted."

So began an enduring rivalry between the brothers that mirrored the parents' differences.

John Neil, known just as "Neil" or by his nickname, "Moon," was always at odds with his mother. But he took after Jack, even parting his hair like his dark, muscular father. Jack, born John Edward Reagan, loved brash laughter and good stories. So did Neil. Jack also loved sports and the heritage of his Irish immigrant father. So did Neil, who was athletic and well-built.

Dreamy and Quiet

Dutch got into his share of boyish trouble and played rough games, like football. But mostly he lived in a "world of pretend," as he later said, in which he would talk to himself and act out little plays he had imagined. He was nearsighted and thin, the dreamy and quiet one.

Ronald "Dutch" Reagan (next to mother) at age 2 with parents
Jack and Nelle and older brother Neil "Moon" Reagan. This
picture was taken in 1913, when the Reagan family lived in
Tampico, Illinois. (Wisconsin Center for Film and Theater
Research.)

Nelle's staid Scotch-English ancestry, her prayers, and her highminded talk appealed to Dutch. In addition to his mother, he got along well with his aunt and teachers. Most women liked him. A well-mannered boy, he always took his hat off as soon as he entered a room.

At age 11, Dutch accepted the Disciples church. Neil, however, rejected the Disciples church for his father's Catholicism when he was 18 years old. Nelle broke down and cried when she was told.

Despite their many differences — religious and otherwise — Nelle kept the family together. Neither Moon nor Dutch would ever feel very close to each other or to Jack. Moon would one day say:

> I knew when [Dutch] had down moments, but I never said anything to him. There was no thought of, you know, putting my arm around his shoulder and saying, 'Let's talk this over,' or anything like that. . . . I always operate on the theory that [Dutch] doesn't even know I'm breathing — but that's the way it's always been with my dad, [Dutch] and myself. Not my mother. She was not that way at all.

During times of togetherness, evenings in Tampico might be spent with a bowl of buttered popcorn in the middle of the table while Jack read the newspaper and Nelle read the *Three Musketeers* to the boys.

An Eyesight Problem

Nelle, born Nelle Clyde Wilson, made education a part of home life, though she, as the youngest of seven children, had never attended high school. Jack, orphaned at six, had gone to work in his aunt and uncle's general store at age 12, ending his schooling at the sixth grade. Nelle wanted more for her children. She had Dutch reading by age five.

Nelle also conveyed a love of drama to her younger son, who sometimes tagged along when she gave local dramatic readings of poetry, plays, and classical speeches "with the zeal of a frustrated actress," Dutch recalled.

In grammar school Dutch did well. But his poor eyesight prevented him from seeing what was on the blackboard. He could not see anything except "colored blobs," he said, but a photographic memory helped him get by. He once amazed his third-grade teacher by rattling off dates and quickly doing multiplication and division problems.

Only at 13 did Dutch try on a pair of glasses to discover excitedly "a glorious, sharply outlined world," as he later said. Nelle got him huge black-rimmed spectacles, but, feeling self-conscious about his appearance, Dutch rarely wore them. Whenever he could, he would slip back into the world of fuzziness. All his life, Ronald Reagan hated wearing glasses.

DIXON— THE "PLACE FOR ME"

Jack took a detour on the way from Tampico to Dixon on that December in 1920, traveling via Galena Street to pass under a wooden arch recently built in honor of the city's World War I heroes. "D I X O N," it said. Beyond and around the landmark stood Dixon, a town of luncheonettes, a drug store with a soda fountain, a movie theater, and a golf course. Its commerce consisted of a cement plant, grain elevators, and other industry supported by the area's rich dairies and farms. The people earned modest wages and lived in plain frame houses. They had grown up there and stayed.

For Dutch, a boy whose family had often moved, Dixon would provide the missing anchor in his life. "All of us have a place to go back to. Dixon is that place for me," Reagan wrote later. "There was the life that has shaped my mind and body for all the years to come after."

In Dixon Dutch met the sweetheart he would keep through college and learned the lessons of small town life — about the basic goodness of people and of sticking together during hard times. He never lost this outlook. After the Reagans drove into Dixon, it became home until age 21 for Dutch, but it has been his hometown ever since.

Money Problems

On entering the city, Jack turned the car down tree-lined South Hennepin Avenue, pulling up before the house at 816, which he had rented for $23 a month, expensive for Dixon. The two-story, white house with a porch across the entryway looked much like the other boxy middle-class houses on the narrow street. It had three bedrooms and a barn in back where Dutch would one day display his collection of birds' eggs. The house was among the better residences the family enjoyed, but it would not be long before financial problems would force them out.

Jack had been made a partner in the Fashion Boot Shop, and he hoped it would bring him good fortune. However, the deal turned out to be less profitable than he had anticipated, leaving him with a low salary. To keep down household costs, Nelle gave up such delicacies as chicken on Sundays, buying liver instead, then considered a pet food, and soup bones. Things did not improve, in part because of Jack's drinking and in part because of the Great Depression. The collapse of the national economy in 1929 wiped out all of Jack's hopes of ever being successful.

Less than three years after moving to Hennepin Avenue, the Reagan family had to find smaller and cheaper accommodations. They would live in five places during their years in Dixon, all of them rented. They almost always bought used cars and went without simple luxuries that most others took for granted. This never seemed strange to Dutch, however. "We didn't know we were poor because the people around us were of the same circumstance," he said.

Lifeguard Hero

In 1924 Dutch entered North Dixon High School. He put little emphasis on academics (earning a low "B" average) but excelled at extracurricular activities, especially drama. From age 15, he worked for seven summers as a lifeguard at Lowell Park, bordering the Rock River, which ran through Dixon on its way to the Mississippi. For $15–20 a week and all the hamburgers and nickel root beers he could consume, Dutch worked at least 12 hours a day for seven days a week.

Sitting in the lifeguard's chair, girls often flocked around. Dutch was on stage. He loved to be looked at, to have a position of authority. He liked the chances to be a hero. During these summers, Dutch saved 77 swimmers. The *Daily Telegraph* chronicled these rescues, which Dutch would track with notches carved in a log near the lifeguard's chair.

People often asked the tanned and good-looking lifeguard about his scorecard, saying, "How many you got now?"

"You count 'em," Dutch would reply.

A Dislike of Indiscipline

Only one person Dutch saved ever thanked him. This may have been because he looked down on the people he rescued, faulting them for lack of discipline. Often they had disregarded warnings about the deep water.

This dislike of indisciplined behavior grew in part out of his father's drinking, which was etched in Dutch's memory by harsh experience. One day when he was 11 years old, the same year he accepted Christianity, Dutch came home to find Jack "flat on his back on the front porch," drunk and smelling of whiskey. "I wanted to let myself in the house and go to bed and pretend he wasn't there," Dutch remembered. No one was around to help, so, full of resentment, self-pity, and grief, he grabbed Jack's overcoat and dragged him inside the house. It was a scene that became a focal point of an autobiography Dutch would write many decades later.

At times like the one on the porch, Dutch would think of his mother. Nelle "told Neil and myself over and over that alcoholism was a sickness — that we should love and help our father and never condemn him for something that was beyond his control," Reagan recalled. His mother "just refused to give up, no matter how dark things looked." From Nelle, Dutch acquired the strength to overcome hardship.

Overwhelming Charm

Dutch did learn some good things from Jack. In his autobiography he writes of times when his father set an example for him and Moon by vigorously denouncing groups like the racist Ku Klux Klan and welcoming into their home black players on Dutch's college football team.

On the whole, however, Jack's drunkenness hurt his sons. He paid little attention to their successes. They built defenses against humiliation: Moon had his flurry of friendships; Dutch learned self-control. He also put his energy into earning respect, acting graciously and responsibly. And his charm was overwhelming. "Look people straight in the eye," Nelle advised. "Remember people's names. Let them know you care." He did. He always said "God bless you" when leaving people.

Dutch was seen as a God-fearing, pious Christian determined to choose the right path. His girlfriend's father, a minister in the Disciples church, hoped he would join the ministry.

Chapter 2
Where Everything Good Began

"Do the duck waddle." Freshman college student Dutch Reagan had ended up on the bottom of the pile again, missing the play in football practice. He could hardly be expected to do otherwise. Reagan was so nearsighted without his horn-rimmed glasses that he could hardly see the ball moving toward him from only a few feet away.

When Coach Ralph McKinzie told Dutch to "duck waddle," he and the other lesser stars of the Eureka College football team started across the field in a squatting position. "Turn around and go back," McKinzie ordered when they reached the goal line.

Reagan headed back. After a hard day's practice, some gave up. But Reagan never quit. He was dogged, determined. Most of all, he had a dream. Dutch wanted more than anything else to follow his hero, former North Dixon High School team captain Garland Waggoner, to football fame. Since age 14, Dutch had been saving his money to attend Eureka College, in Eureka, Illinois, over 100 miles south of Dixon, where Waggoner had gone on to become a football star. At 18, there was no doubt in Reagan's mind about what he wanted.

INSPIRED BY HEROS

In the fall of 1928, Reagan headed off to Eureka College inspired by many heroes, real and imaginary, who would shape his life. "I'm a sucker for hero worship," he would write nearly 50 years later. As a child he read books about athletes, soldiers, Presidents, and achievers who started with nothing and became industrial giants or public servants. "My reading left an abiding belief in the triumph of good over evil," he wrote of these books. "There were heroes who lived by standards of morality and fair play." He would choose the theme of heroism at his presidential oath-taking ceremony in 1981, telling listeners that Americans had "every right to dream heroic dreams."

The college football dream, however, went badly at first. Dutch had gone from first-string guard on his high school team to fifth-string in a school of about 220 students, only half of them male. He did not play in a single game the whole first year. Once, when the team took a group picture and was short a jersey, Dutch was the one excluded from the picture. He blamed the coach. "I told everyone who would listen that the coach didn't like me," Reagan said. He almost refused to return to college for his second year, he was so disappointed.

EUREKA COLLEGE

Reagan had not expected disappointment when he first arrived at Eureka. Walking up the path to the campus for the first time to begin his freshman year, Dutch's desire to attend Eureka was confirmed. He fell in love with the college. Its rolling green lawns, huge shady elms, and semicircle of five main buildings seemed like "another home," he recalled. In a way, it was. The red-brick, ivy-covered institution grew out of the vision of pioneers who belonged to the Disciples church. Religious values and attitudes Nelle taught at home were seen as part of everything from sports to homework at Eureka.

It was these values and attitudes that set Eureka apart from other colleges. In those days, other colleges around the nation were experiencing the youthful rebellion of the "Roaring Twenties," with campus crazes for raccoon coats, dancing, and what for the time were shockingly short dresses (above the knees). Despite the 1920–1933 constitutional ban on alcohol called "Prohibition," alcohol drinking was common at most colleges. But not at Eureka. There, dancing and drinking were frowned upon and chapel attendance required. The dress code forbade dresses exposing the calf. Yet, while in some ways tame, the college faced its own brand of rebelliousness.

A Financial Crisis

When Reagan became a freshman, the institution was facing a financial crisis. The money problems stemmed in part from the looming Depression. It would begin for most of the country with the stock market crash of 1929 but had begun in the Corn Belt a year earlier. College President Bert Wilson carefully worked out a plan to economize by combining departments. That's when the trouble began.

The faculty resisted, focusing its rancor on Wilson, who had, with the board of trustees' support, called for the cutbacks. Students, apparently out of sympathy for their teachers, took up the cause, though the plan would not directly affect them. They petitioned and then went out on a 10-day strike which led to Wilson's resignation.

This protest took on special importance for Reagan. As a member of the Tau Kappa Epsilon fraternity, the organization leading the protest, he was swept up in the strike.

A Freshman Spokesman

Though the hour was near midnight, students clanged the college bell for 15 minutes, waking the sleeping town, calling its students, teachers, and townspeople to the chapel. People came from all directions, many still wearing nightclothes under their overcoats. They filled the room and overflowed into the aisles and doorways. The crisis brewing in recent days at the college was coming to a head.

A committee of students huddled on the sidelines, hammering out details of a statement they had called the community together to hear: "We, the students of Eureka College, on the 28th of November, 1928, declare an immediate strike pending the acceptance of [Eureka College] President Wilson's resignation by the board of trustees." For 2½ hours, speakers went before the crowd to debate the proposal.

In Reagan's version of the events, he appears as a spokesman for the student strike committee. He was a freshman representative on the committee and, self-admittedly, "far from a ringleader." He said he mounted the platform and spoke against the deviousness of the board of trustees. He condemned their vote to carry out a drastic academic cutback, saying that it would hurt students. The crowd was swept up in a wave of defiance. When the time came to present the strike motion, Dutch's speech brought the audience to their feet, roaring with approval, he said.

A Moment to Remember

It was a moment Reagan would always remember. "I discovered that night," he was to say, "that an audience has a feel to it and, in the parlance of the theater, that audience and I were together." Seeing the crowd react "was heady wine," he said. He drew from the strike, in which students brought down a college president, "an education in human nature and the rights of man to universal education."

But judging by his autobiographical recollection of the conflict, Reagan apparently misunderstood much of what was going on. In his telling, the strike succeeded. "It was our policy of polite resistance that brought victory," he wrote. In fact, the outcome changed little and the student activism proved pointless. The president's resignation was probably unwarranted, and the cutbacks went ahead anyway. Reagan's account neglects to mention the students' eventual retraction of all of their demands.

Whatever the facts, Dutch found something important for himself: a place on the side of righteousness, a place for passionate views, for sermons, for causes in which he could believe. It was a role he would play again and again in later life. Reagan would look back on the strike as a foretaste of his future involvement in politics.

SWEET COLLEGE LIFE

After the strike, Reagan's years at Eureka passed in a blur of happy activity. On returning for his second year, he met with better luck on the football team and also joined the swimming team. During his college years, he became president of the Booster Club, edited the yearbook, and served as a member of student senate and senior class president. He worked at dishwashing jobs and waiting tables on and off campus to earn what his partial football scholarship and summer savings could not cover of room, board, and the $180 tuition.

The fraternity boys never lacked for fun, pulling pranks on the freshmen or holding dances. On weekends, Dutch dated fellow student Margaret "Muggs" Cleaver, the minister's daughter he had dated at North Dixon High School.

His relationship with Margaret made the college years particularly happy, but the couple had basic differences. Margaret excelled at academics. She was curious and studious. She wanted to see the world. Dutch did poorly in his classes, barely passing with a string of Cs. He chose economics as a major because the professor who taught the subject was an easy grader. When Dutch studied, rather than trying to understand the material, he would memorize it to pass the tests.

Interest in Drama

Had he applied himself, Dutch could have done better, Margaret always thought. Even so, "I didn't think he'd end up accomplishing anything," she said. Dutch's energy went into outside pursuits, such as drama.

Reagan had studied drama in high school with drama coach B. J. Frazer, from whom he said later he "learned almost everything I know about acting." Frazer made his students "think our roles instead of acting them out mechanically," Dutch wrote. Frazer said he would sit a cast down and ask, "Why, why, why are the characters doing these things?" When the students got on stage, they were the characters.

In college, under drama coach Ellen Marie Johnson, Dutch acted in seven plays. The highlight of his college acting career came when he was part of a Eureka troupe competing in a Northwestern University contest. The troupe, including Margaret, won third place for the play *Aria da Capo*. Reagan won an honorable mention for his portrayal of a shepherd boy.

Football Jock

Dutch had returned to college for his second year feeling angry. "I . . . had decided the only way to revenge myself on Mac [the coach] was to make the team," he said. He also had

Dutch Reagan shows off his football form at Eureka College, where he played on the college team. (National Archives, Reagan Presidential Material Staff).

another motivation that year. Moon, who had taken a job in a cement plant after high school, came to Eureka on a scholarship arranged with Dutch's help. The arrival of Moon, who was by far the better football player, aroused the old rivalry between the two brothers.

"Dutch did better once Moon was on the team," McKinzie said. "Seemed he had to prove himself more." Dutch came to admire Coach McKinzie, whom he credits with motivating him to perform. In his last three years, Dutch became a solid player but never a star. He is most remembered for his antics. He "used to take an old broom from the locker room and pretend it was a microphone and 'announce' the game play by play afterwards. Never forgot a play either!" McKinzie recalled. He also said that Dutch understood the game better than most players.

THE DEPRESSION HITS HOME

In 1928, President Herbert Hoover had declared, "I have no fears for the future of our country." He soon appeared out of touch. The stock market crashed in 1929, triggering the Great Depression. In that year, unemployment jumped to four million and the number of people on relief shot up 200 percent. By 1932, 13 million people, one out of every four workers, had no jobs, and of those still working, many had reduced wages, hours, or both.

But Dutch managed to get by. He kept his summer job as a lifeguard during college, and Eureka College came up with financial aid to keep him in school.

The meaning of the Depression struck home, however, while on a football trip to Springfield, Illinois. Dutch and Moon convinced Coach McKinzie to let them visit their father, who had closed the Fashion Boot Shop in Dixon in 1931 and taken a job in Springfield, 145 miles to the south. What they found shocked them into understanding.

Jack was the "sole clerk of this hole-in-the wall with its garish orange paper ads plastered over the windows and front and one cheap bench with iron armrests to separate the customers, if there was more than one at a time," Dutch wrote. Nelle had taken a job as a seamstress in order to make ends meet. Without Jack's knowledge, Dutch sent $50 home to Nelle from money he saved from dishwashing.

Fear at Graduation

By 1932, Dutch's graduating class had shrunk as financial pressures forced students to drop out of school. The threat of unemployment loomed large. At the sunny June 7 graduation ceremony that year, Eureka's new president, Clyde Lyon, insisted in his address to the students that they not let the bleak-looking future "bully them into non-achievement."

As part of the ceremony, the 45 graduates stood in a circle holding a woven ivy chain clipped from the ivy that grew on the college buildings. All but those who wanted to be recognized as couples were to break the chain in a symbolic farewell to Eureka. Margaret and Dutch stayed attached.

The college years had come to an end. Dutch, however, would return to Eureka many times, one day to receive an honorary degree and to joke, "I thought my first Eureka degree was an honorary one." On October 17, 1980, Reagan stopped there while on a presidential campaign swing. With obvious joy at returning, he told the cheering students, "As far as I am concerned, everything good that has happened to me – everything – started here on this campus in those four years that are still such a part of my life."

Chapter 3
Riding the Radio Waves

"This Depression isn't going to last forever and smart businessmen are willing to take on young men who can learn their business in order to have trained manpower on hand when things start to roll," said Sid Altschuler, father of one of the beach-going families at Lowell Park in Dixon. He and Dutch were sitting together one summer evening of 1932 on the edge of the pier. "What do you think you'd like to do?" Altschuler asked.

Dutch drew a blank. After graduation, he had gone back to work as a lifeguard for the last time. He was wondering what he would do in the fall. He knew he had a talent for communication but could not decide how he could use those skills. Altschuler waited while Dutch thought.

"I don't know," Dutch finally said.

But Dutch was encouraged by the man's remark. He called it "literally the first note of optimism I had heard about the state of the nation." Altschuler promised to help him get a job. For days Dutch thought about what type of work he wanted. He knew he wanted "some form of show business" but he did not think he had any chance of getting directly into the field. He chose a radio broadcasting career as the next best.

"Well, you've picked a line in which I have no connections," Altschuler later told Dutch. But he encouraged him. "You've picked a sound industry . . . start knocking on doors, tell anyone who'll listen that you believe you have a future in the business, and you'll take any kind of job, even sweeping floors, just to get in."

Dutch took the fatherly advice. He planned to hitchhike to Chicago, the center of the new radio industry in the Midwest, to look for a job. Before the trip he stopped in Eureka to visit Margaret, whose family had moved there in 1931 when her father, Ben Cleaver, became the college pastor. Dutch, perhaps lacking close ties to his own father, looked up to older men like Cleaver and Altschuler.

Dutch said good-bye to Margaret, who had a teaching job lined up for the fall. They were expected to marry, but all Dutch could think about that fall was getting a job. "A job, any job, seemed like the ultimate success," he wrote. His relationship with Margaret had to wait.

BOTTOMING OUT

It was 1932, the bottom of the Depression. The Democratic presidential candidate, New York Governor Franklin Delano Roosevelt, would run with the promise of government-sponsored aid to farmers, small businesses, and the millions of unemployed. He campaigned from a wheelchair, which he had to use because his legs had been crippled by polio. When, with the help of his son, he stood up to call for a "New Deal," a federal action plan to revive America, crowds cheered. They were ready for change.

Many blamed the nation's state of affairs on President Hoover, a Republican whose re-election campaign was met with rotten eggs, tomatoes, and chants of "hang Hoover."

Hoover and many more fortunate Americans feared aid programs and change might make matters worse. Dutch sided
with Roosevelt, who inspired hope in him and many others.
In those bleak times, hope was badly needed.

The Big Break

Dutch had had it. After being turned down again and again
by radio stations in Chicago and getting swollen feet from
walking city sidewalks, he heeded advice to look for work
in smaller cities, where stations were willing to give a new-
comer a chance. He drove to Davenport, Iowa, 65 miles west
of Dixon, to give it a try but met with yet another refusal.
He could not hold back his disappointment. "How . . . does
a guy ever get to be a sports announcer if he can't get inside
a [radio] station," he grumbled as he took his leave from program manager Peter MacArthur, who had interviewed him
at station WOC in Davenport.

Dutch started to leave, but the Scottish-American interviewer perked up at the mention of sports. He called Dutch
back.

"Do ye think ye could tell me about a game and make
me see it? I mean really see it, so as I'd know what was goin'
on?" he said.

"I think I could," said Dutch.

MacArthur led Dutch to a studio soundproofed with
heavy blue velvet drapes. Reagan was left alone to announce
an imaginary game while MacArthur listened outside. Dutch
quickly conjured up the cliff-hanger final quarter of a football game Eureka had played, narrating it moment by moment. He improved his own role, blocking the linebacker he
had missed in the real game. After 20 minutes, he reached
Eureka's last-minute win and wound up with, "We return you
now to our main studio." He was dripping with sweat when
MacArthur came back in.

The program manager liked what he had heard. He hired Reagan on the spot to announce a forthcoming University of Iowa football game for five dollars and bus fare. This was the foot in the door Reagan needed to win his hoped-for job.

But it was not a permanent job. After Dutch broadcast his first game, demonstrating his grasp of football and his ability to recreate the game for radio audiences, MacArthur offered him three more Saturday games at $10 each and bus fare. These four games were Reagan's only employment for five months. He was, for the first time, unemployed.

Sometime near Christmas, probably in 1932, just after Roosevelt was elected, the Depression reached its bleakest point for the Reagans. As Dutch and Moon were going out on dates, a special delivery letter arrived at the family's two-room apartment. Jack opened it and, without raising his head, said, "Well, it's a [heck] of a Christmas present." The delivery was a blue slip informing Jack that he had been fired.

Fear of Fear Itself

In February 1933, would-be assassin Giuseppe Zangara tried to shoot Roosevelt, but missed. Roosevelt was sworn in under tight security a few days later, saying in his speech to the nation, that "the only thing we have to fear is fear itself—nameless, unjustified terror." The President worked quickly to put his New Deal rescue plan into effect.

Within days, Roosevelt sought to win over the public with the first regular presidential use of radio. His broadcast of "fireside chats" set a pattern many later Presidents would imitate. "My friends, I want to talk to you for a few minutes . . .," Roosevelt would say in his aristocratic accent as he began to discuss banking or other problems of the day. Reagan would, as President, adopt the fireside chat format, too, speaking over radio more than any President since Roosevelt.

Reagan's affection for Roosevelt set him apart in those times. Most Dixonites had supported the Republicans and Hoover, but Jack was a fervent Democrat. He had toiled during the summer of 1932 in Democratic headquarters in Dixon to drum up votes for Roosevelt. Dutch, voting in a presidential election for the first time, followed Jack and cast his vote for Roosevelt, who would win a huge victory. The triumph had direct benefits for the Reagans.

In June 1933, Jack was rewarded for his support of the Democrats with a job administering one of the local work-relief programs. It helped him win back some of his lost self-respect. He drank less. Moon, through his father's influence, also obtained a government job. Dutch, who years later in his political life, would condemn government welfare programs, now felt grateful, seeing Roosevelt as a family savior.

From WOC to WHO

Around Christmas of 1932, program manager MacArthur, who would become Dutch Reagan's boss, mentor, and father figure of the period (Reagan would call him "a saint, but a show business kind of saint"), offered Dutch a job as a WOC staff announcer for $100 a month—a hefty salary in those days. He took the job and moved to Davenport, a city of about 75,000 people.

Dutch began work in February 1933, finding his radio announcing job somewhat less thrilling than expected. He spent most of his time as a disc jockey filling in between reading commercials. In May, however, WOC was merged into Radio WHO in Des Moines, Iowa, a city twice as large as Davenport. WHO was a key station in the NBC network and Reagan became its chief sports announcer, doubling his salary. He called home to tell Nelle and Margaret the good news.

Margaret had some news for Dutch, too. She told him

As the sports announcer for Radio WHO, in Des Moines, Iowa, Dutch Reagan honed his speaking skills and became a local celebrity. (National Archives, Reagan Presidential Material Staff.)

that she was going to spend a year in France with her sister as soon as the school year was over.

"Where does that leave us?" he asked.

"With time to find ourselves," she said.

A RADIO CELEBRITY

Reagan had entered broadcasting at a time when radio reached millions of listeners and television was still years away. WHO, a 50,000-watt station, broadcast from Des Moines to the Midwest all the popular radio programming of the 1930s, from comedy shows to sports, news, and farm service information.

Reagan quickly became a local celebrity. He interviewed sports and film stars who came through the city, wrote a sports column, and spoke at civic occasions. He was most proud of his main job, announcing sports, especially baseball. He announced more than 600 games by recreating them from brief messages telegraphed to him in Des Moines. To fill in between messages, Reagan would make up what he thought the player was probably doing. He added crowd sounds by moving a foot pedal.

Once, during a Chicago Cubs–St. Louis Cardinals game, the wire went dead. Reagan, wanting to keep up the radio fakery to prevent the audience from tuning to another station, continued to create an imaginary game for more than six minutes, reporting on the hitter's foul balls (which are not recorded) and describing in detail the "red-headed kid who had scrambled and gotten the souvenir ball." No one objected when he invented game action. It was part of the way sports was covered. Reagan learned that audiences cared more for drama than accuracy. This was a lesson he would carry into politics.

News from France

Though he had not accepted the possibility that he and Margaret might have broken up for good, Dutch went out with other women. A year after Margaret went to France, she wrote that she planned to marry an American diplomat she had met. Dutch was shocked. About the same time news came that Jack had suffered a heart attack. Jack survived, but could no longer work. Fortunately, Dutch found himself in a favorable position to cope with these events.

Dutch had been sending money home ever since he obtained his radio job. By now he was comfortable sending $25 a week to Nelle. He also helped Moon pay his college tuition and, later, helped him get a job as an announcer at WHO. By husbanding his income carefully, avoiding buying on credit and never letting others pay for him at a restaurant, Dutch had money to spare and the freedom to spend a bit on himself.

He enjoyed his new station in life, buying himself a two-seater, brown convertible with his savings. It matched his suits and tobacco pipe. He became one of Des Moines's most eligible bachelors.

Friends recall how Dutch and his dates would make the rounds of the city's fanciest night clubs — Cy's Moonlight Inn was his favorite. He also joined the U.S. Cavalry Reserve in nearby Camp Dodge, which enabled him to receive weekend training in horsemanship. So began a lifelong interest in horses.

"Rendezvous with Destiny"

The times were still hard, however. Dust storms that swept across the Great Plains brought new misery, displacing thousands of farmers. Roosevelt's New Deal had not ended poverty or unemployment, but millions were better off in 1936 than in 1932. The banks were again stable and other reforms accomplished. When the Democrats renominated Roosevelt in 1936, he reviewed the progress of his term, declaring, "This generation of Americans has a rendezvous with destiny."

Reagan felt closer than ever to Roosevelt. That fall he would plug the Democrats at every opportunity on the radio. When Roosevelt came through Des Moines on a campaign tour, Dutch rushed to the window in excitement to glimpse his hero waving to crowds. He imitated Roosevelt's fireside chats for friends and celebrated his re-election.

The New Deal: A "Let's See What Works" Approach

On accepting his party's nomination for President in 1932, Franklin D. Roosevelt told the delegates at the Democratic National Convention, "I pledge you, I pledge myself, to a new deal for the American people." The words "new deal" came to represent an array of measures Roosevelt set in motion after taking office in 1933.

The New Deal programs lacked a consistent philosophy. They were a "let's see what works" approach to the Depression, characterized by an openness to new ideas and a willingness to use and expand federal powers to achieve their ends. These ends included relief for the needy, reform of economic institutions, and relief from economic crisis for the nation at large.

The various programs led to the establishment of many federal agencies to provide employment, welfare and other assistance to millions of people. These efforts, however, did not go far enough. Programs such as the Works Progress Administration (WPA), responsible for make-work projects ranging from playground building to federal funding for artists, failed to reach some seven million of the unemployed.

Despite this weakness, the New Deal left significant legacies. It benefited labor, allowing unions to expand and establishing new standards for minimum wages and working hours. It set up government bodies to regulate the stock exchanges and help prevent bank panics like the ones that helped spark the Depression.

The New Deal created the Social Security Act of 1935 to involve the government in areas such as old-age pensions, unemployment insurance, and assistance to the needy. The act became a basis for later expansion of a number of federally assisted social services and led, in part, to the buildup of "big government" that Ronald Reagan would one day oppose.

HOLLYWOOD, HERE I COME!

Dutch was looking to the future. By 1936 he knew better where his abilities lay: in his soothing voice, his charm, and his way with people. Contacts with celebrities fueled his dream of becoming an actor. He learned that he might be able to make it in Hollywood if he would just go there and meet influential people.

Dutch managed to get the radio station to send him on his vacation time to California to cover the Cubs winter practice on Catalina Island, off Los Angeles. He went there in February 1937, half-heartedly reporting on the games while trying to set up a screen test at a movie studio.

Nothing much happened until Dutch contacted Joy Hodges, a rising band singer from Des Moines and a former WHO performer whom he had interviewed at WHO. "He confessed he wanted a movie test. . . . I asked him to stand up and remove his glasses: he did and it was clear that he was *very handsome.* I told him never to put those glasses on again," she recalled. Hodges arranged for a meeting with a talent agent.

The agent saw that Reagan was a "type," the "likeable, clean-cut American" with sex appeal and charm. Dutch exaggerated his experience, doubling his salary at WHO and turning the Eureka drama club into the "The Johnson Professional Players" (after the college drama coach). The bogus group would later be listed on his studio biography and in press releases.

Successful Screen Test

A screen test at Warner Brothers studios was arranged. Reagan did a scene opposite June Travis from the play "Holiday" and then took the train back to Iowa. He reported to work on the following Monday, ready to laugh off the whole thing. Then, around lunch, a telegram arrived from the agent:

WARNERS OFFER CONTRACT SEVEN YEARS, ONE YEAR'S OPTION, STARTING AT $200 A WEEK. WHAT SHALL I DO?

Dutch excitedly sent his acceptance and wired the good news to Joy Hodges. She sent another telegram to the Des Moines *Register*:

POTENTIAL STAR IN YOUR MIDST. DUTCH REAGAN LOCAL SPORTS ANNOUNCER SIGNED LONG TERM WARNER BROTHERS CONTRACT . . . THEY CONSIDER HIM GREATEST BET SINCE [HOLLYWOOD STAR ROBERT] TAYLOR WITHOUT GLASSES.

The WHO crew gave Dutch an on-the-air send-off party, attended by the mayor. Afterwards, he piled his belongings into his convertible and headed west. From June 1, 1937, Dutch would be known to moviegoers by his Hollywood name: Ronald Reagan.

Chapter 4

To the Brink of Stardom

To his co-workers and friends, he was "Ronnie Reagan," a fellow who wore thick glasses off the set and loved to talk about weighty subjects. Actor Larry Williams recalled, "Ronnie might . . . [sit] down next to you . . . [and] suddenly [say] something like, 'Larry, before I run down for you this Far Eastern concept I'm sort of kicking around in my mind, answer me a background question: What would you say is the current population of Formosa [Taiwan]?'

" 'Ronnie, I don't know things like that.'

" 'Right. Most Americans don't. No need to apologize.'

" 'I'm glad.'

" 'I've got the figure right here, but before I give it to you maybe I should just jog your memory a bit about Chinese history in the last three thousand years.' "

A PASSION FOR POLITICS

Reagan's passion for politics set him apart; it seemed to surpass even his devotion to acting. He would work hard, accepting long and tiring acting assignments, never refusing a role and, unlike the more temperamental actors, never making trouble for the directors. He rarely questioned how to interpret a script or scene. But he asked little of himself as an actor. Other actors devoted themselves to their craft, taking lessons outside or working with a theater group to hone their skills. Not Reagan. In acting, he was satisfied with his natural ability.

After settling into his new job, Reagan sent for his parents, who now depended on him for their livelihood. He found Nelle and Jack a ground-floor apartment in West Hollywood, where he visited them often. He had not attended church in Des Moines, but now he went with Nelle.

Marriage to Jane Wyman

Ronald dated some of the actresses from the studio, but nothing serious developed until 1938. For a film promotion for "Brother Rat," he was called on to pose for pictures with actress Jane Wyman. Due to a scheduling mixup, they had a long wait for the photographer. Jane resented the delay, feeling sure someone was pushing them around.

"It's just a mistake," Ronald said. "It's no one's fault. No one would inconvenience us on purpose."

Jane, who had been attracted to Reagan's sunny personality on the set, wondered if what she viewed as "easy good nature" could be an "act." How could a man have "so even a disposition consistently?" she wondered.

Ronald asked Jane for a date. They were soon dating regularly.

An Ambitious Woman

Three years younger than Reagan, Jane was an ambitious, driven woman, determined to achieve stardom. With her brown hair bleached platinum, she played the empty-headed blonde in films.

Born Sarah Jane Fulks before taking her stage name of

Jane Wyman, she had had a fairly unhappy childhood in California and Missouri, dropped out of high school to get a job, and worked her way into films as a dancer in a studio chorus line. When she met Reagan, she was in the process of getting a divorce after a 17-month marriage.

To Wyman, a woman full of anger and suspicion, Ronald brought a feeling of safety. "For the first time in my life I truly trusted someone," she said. Ronnie felt protective toward her. They married on January 26, 1940.

The marriage of the two Hollywood stars attracted a flurry of news coverage by a press eager to see the union as a "good-guy-tames-wild-blonde-and-lives-happily-ever-after" story. In the news and gossip columns, the marriage would be treated like a real-life fairy tale.

Star of the B's

After a honeymoon in Palm Springs, California, both Jane and Ronnie resumed making films. Jane, who had had a harder time breaking into movies than Ronnie, was the more aggressive in pursuing her career goals. Reagan was often cast as the earnest-but-not-too-bright romantic leading male who usually got the girl. He did best in roles as the sincere, likeable type, similar to Robert Taylor, to whom he had been compared.

Reagan, however, thought of himself as "the Errol Flynn of the B's," just as brave as the swashbuckling film star, but in low-budget pictures. In one series of war movies, he starred as Lieutenant "Brass" Bancroft, protecting a secret "inertia projector" weapon from those who would steal it from the U.S. government. Such roles won him recognition. Reagan was not a top star, but well up in a second level of "contract players" cultivated by the studio for possible stardom.

Ronnie came to see his casting as limiting, but he did little about it until he married Wyman. He wanted to play roles that would launch him into stardom. When it was announced that a football film called "Life of Knute Rockne" (later changed to "Knute Rockne—All American") was to be made, Reagan wanted a part. He felt it would advance his career. Encouraged by Jane, for the first time he lobbied for a part and got it.

"One for the Gipper"

The film recounts the story of the Notre Dame University football coach, Knute Rockne. Reagan plays the coach's star player, George Gipp, who performs heroic football feats, winning games for Notre Dame until his death at age 20 of pneumonia. Reagan's most memorable line as Gipp, nicknamed "the Gipper," is said on his deathbed to Rockne (played by Pat O'Brien), when he asks the coach to "win one for the Gipper."

Eight years after Gipp's death, Rockne used the line in a half-time pep talk to a losing Notre Dame football team divided by bickering and jealousy. He rallied the players to win. It made for great drama, but some doubt persists about whether the line was ever uttered by Gipp. More likely, it was invented by Rockne, who often motivated teams with locker room stories he dreamed up.

Even so, Reagan's "Gipper" line would stick with him all the way to the White House, where one of his nicknames would be "the Gipper."

The film premiered in October 1940 in South Bend, Indiana, home of Notre Dame. Reagan attended the opening-night festivities with Jane and his father, even though he worried that Jack would embarrass him by drinking too much. Jack did get drunk, but avoided notice. The premiere went well and the movie won praise. It proved to be one of the most successful of the Reagan films.

The trip to South Bend turned out to be a last fling for Jack, who died on May 18, 1941. What Reagan called Jack's

In a scene from the 1940 movie "Knute Rockne-All American," Reagan, as George Gipp, speaks with Pat O'Brien, who played Knute Rockne. The film was one of the high points of Reagan's acting career. (Turner Entertainment Co.)

"black curse" and the "chilling fear" that Jack would humiliate him were now also dead.

A Visit to Dixon

Reagan stepped up to the microphone before an estimated 35,000 people chanting, "We love Dutch." He looked out at the "WELCOME HOME DUTCH!" banners and at the crowd gathered at the Dixon train station on September 14, 1941. He then raised his hand to quiet the throng. "I do not feel at ease on this platform," he said, blushing noticeably. "I would rather be out at Lowell Park beach calling to the kids to quit rocking the raft." The remark prompted a wave of shouting and applause.

Reagan had returned a proud local hero on a celebrity tour in honor of another Dixonite, Hollywood gossip columnist Luella Parsons. The town had declared a holiday in her honor, and she had returned with famous actors and comedians standing on the platform with her that morning. To her annoyance, Reagan stole the show. At the microphone, he went on reminiscing about his days in Dixon until Parsons stepped in to reclaim centerstage.

One actor in the troupe commented to Parsons, "This fellow must be running for Congress!"

"Where's the Rest of Me?"

Reagan believed he achieved the peak of his acting career in a 1942 drama titled "Kings Row." Reagan was cast as playboy Drake McHugh, the victim in a much-sanitized movie version of the novel of the same name about twisted minds in a small town. In the scene Reagan is most proud of, McHugh discovers his legs have been amputated by a mad doctor angry over McHugh's romance with his daughter.

Reacting in a believable way before camera was a challenge, Reagan wrote. The character had to come "from un-consciousness to full realization of what had happened in a few seconds. . . . Worst of all, I had to give my reaction in a line of no more than five words," he said. "Where's the rest of me?" are the words he delivered and would one day use as the title of his autobiography. Though critics at the time liked the scene, film historians consider Reagan had little tal-ent for giving depth to difficult dramatic roles. But they say he did admirably in parts he found less satisfying: the light, romantic leading man.

RONNIE, JANE, AND POLITICS

In their marriage, Ronnie was the man of the house. He made the decisions; Jane did the decorating. He was the sober, care-ful one, insisting they budget, save, and build for the future. Their first child, Maureen, was born on January 4, 1941.

The Reagans lived in an apartment while looking for a house, but found nothing they liked until they saw the home they wanted in the movie, "This Thing Called Love." They built the eight-room house that appeared in the film. By this time, they could afford more luxurious living, a pair of Scotty dogs named Scotch and Soda (the same as the Roosevelts' dogs), and a taste for fine wines. Their agents had negotiated three-year contracts which rocketed Reagan's salary to $2,750 a week and Wyman's to $2,500.

At parties Jane was full of fun, anxiously so. She seemed to need people's love and approval. Ronnie told stories, often making fun of Jane. He would also get into heavy political arguments with ardent Republican businessmen or with his recently married brother Neil (still known as "Moon"), who had followed him to California in the hopes of breaking into the movies. One businessman was so impressed with Ronald that he offered to help elect him to Congress if he switched to the Republican Party.

An Ardent Democrat

The seed of ambition was planted. But Reagan still favored the Democrats and would try to convert others to his party. Moon, who had joined the Republicans in 1932, recalled conversations they had during this time at parties.

> If they (the party guests) were out around the pool, in 30 minutes the Reagan brothers would have driven everybody into the house with our battles on politics. [Ronald's] statement to me always was, 'That's the trouble with you guys. [You think] anybody who voted for Roosevelt is a Communist,' and I used to agree with him heartily, at which point we'd get the screaming meemies.

Moon's associating the Democrats with the Communists was much the same line taken by all Republicans, who considered themselves the keepers of the American way of life. They saw the Democrats, with the possible exception of Roosevelt himself, as the liberal left being taken over secretly by Communists and their friends. These views reflected the times: war was looming and fear dominated the political scene. Americans saw Nazi and Communist spies, saboteurs, and subversion everywhere. By June of 1940, ordinary American citizens were contacting the U.S. Justice Department with tip-offs at the rate of 3,000 a day.

Pearl Harbor

When Japanese planes attacked Pearl Harbor, Hawaii, on December 7, 1941, the nation mobilized for war in Europe and the Pacific. Reagan was drafted on April 19, 1942, and was stationed with an Air Force unit in Los Angeles. He remained on duty there until the end of the war, making, at Air Force pay, propaganda and patriotic movies like "This Is The Army." The post was assigned to him in part because of his poor vision, which disqualified him from active combat. He had no choice in the assignment.

Life for Reagan went on almost as normal. Most weekdays he lived in army quarters at the studio, but he went home the rest of the time.

Growing Interest in Politics

He may have been at home, but during the war years Ronald's mind was on the military experience. It brought him in closer contact with government officials than ever before. He began to look at government differently.

By the end of the war, when Reagan was discharged from service as a captain, one too many run-ins with what he called "self-serving government bureaucrats" had given him a tarnished, more skeptical view of the federal government. His interest in politics and conservative views grew in proportion.

As Reagan changed, so did the political landscape. Roosevelt, who had won an unprecedented third term in 1944 and led the nation through the war years, died of natural causes on April 12, 1945, just short of seeing the end of World War II. The death hit Reagan deeply, as it did many Americans.

Vice-President Harry Truman, of whom Reagan knew little and whom he would later describe as "inspiring as mud," had taken Roosevelt's place to serve out the term. Truman won re-election in 1948. Reagan voted for him, but it was the last time he would cast his ballot for a Democrat. Without Roosevelt, Reagan felt less tied to the Democratic Party; it would never be the same in his eyes.

Chapter 5

Hollywood Crusades

J ane was woken up again by Ronald. He was already awake, sitting up in bed. Thinking he had heard a noise, possibly an intruder, he had grabbed his gun from the bedside table and held it in readiness. No one. It was nothing, like the other late night alerts, when Ronnie had sat up in bed, gun ready, only to see shadows in the room. They went back to sleep.

Reagan kept the loaded .32 Smith and Wesson with him night and day in much of late 1946. He wore it during waking hours in a shoulder holster. This practice began when a telephone caller had threatened "to fix [his] face so [he] would never be in pictures again" if he opposed unions on strike at the studio. Reagan was not backing down. Believing Communist subversives controlled the strikers as part of a dark political conspiracy, he sided with the studios and a competing union.

FIGHTING THE COMMUNIST CONSPIRACY

To support that side, Reagan had crossed angry lines of picketers and entered studio gates where strikers overturned and set fire to cars as police used tear gas and hoses to quell the violence. Many had been injured. But the battle was waged mostly with words, with Reagan taking a decisive role at its center.

Having become increasingly immersed in politics, Reagan was convinced that the striking union, the Conference of Studio Unions (CSU), was playing the main part in a Communist plot. "The Communists—they were the cause of the labor strife, they used minor jurisdictional disputes [concerning rights to organize] as excuses for their scheme. Their aim was to gain economic control of the motion picture industry in order to finance their activities and subvert the screen for their propaganda," he wrote. He believed the world's future now hung in the balance, as he also wrote:

> In those days before television and massive foreign film production, American films dominated 95 percent of the world's movie screens. We had a weekly audience of about 500,000,000 souls. Takeover of this enormous plant and its gradual transformation into a Communist gristmill was a grandiose [plan]. It would have been a magnificent coup for our enemies.
>
> Using the CSU as a vehicle for Communist aims was a first step of admirable directness.

A Man with a Mission

Reagan believed, along with many other people filled with postwar fears, that Moscow was behind such schemes as the CSU strike. The war-weary Soviet Union may not have been up to world domination, yet Reagan saw the storm in Hollywood as the key in fighting off world enslavement by the Communists and saving the American way of life.

Reagan probably overestimated the threat. The strike was really a matter of the producers and the nonstriking unions working to protect their financial interests. The CSU did have legitimate grievances, and later studies cast doubt on the charge of backstage manipulation by Communists. Members of the Communist Party in the United States may have taken an interest in Hollywood and the CSU, but Reagan and others inflated their importance. All this, Reagan failed to see—for in his opposition to Communism, he felt he was on a mission. It became all he thought about and talked about.

A FIRST STEP

After the war ended, Reagan's film career was going badly. Warner Brothers gave him few movie roles. To fill time late in 1945, he joined voluntary organizations, most notably the Hollywood Independent Citizens Committee of Arts, Sciences and Professions, or HICCASP. The group united people concerned about such issues as the spread of weapons like the atomic bombs the United States dropped on Japan to end the war in the Pacific. Reagan took an active role in HICCASP, speaking publicly on serious issues. It was a first step into the world of politics.

That step led very soon to thorny disputes over the so-called "Red menace" of Communism. Reagan wanted HIC-CASP to reject Communism openly, which would have demonstrated the organization's approval of the wave of anti-Red feeling sweeping the country. The membership watered down the proposal, suggesting to Reagan that the group was influenced by Communists. He shared his concerns with Moon, now an advertising executive, who was working secretly as an informer for the Federal Bureau of Investigation (FBI). Moon had repeatedly urged Ronnie to leave HICCASP.

A Narrow Escape

At midnight one night, Ronald called his brother from a hamburger stand and asked Moon to meet him there. Ronald revealed his suspicions about HICCASP to Moon, who said, "Junior, what do you suppose I've been talking about." Ronald seemed surprised.

"Why, you never mentioned a word about anything like that," Ronald said. Fearing that he might be associated with the Communists, Reagan soon submitted his resignation to HICCASP. Even though he would soon establish himself as a leading anti-Communist, he left just in time. He had narrowly escaped being labeled a "Red sympathizer."

In the late 1940s, showing any signs of less-than-total rejection of Communism or anyone remotely connected with it, even unknowingly, could be dangerous. Not opposing Communism strongly enough was considered a basis for suspicion. During the postwar years, an estimated 2,000 people with ties to the film studios would be secretly black- or gray-listed—excluded or restricted—from work for years for suspected ties to the Communist Party. However, less than one percent were ever proven party members. Most were liberals and patriotic Americans who fell victim to false accusations, "Red-baiting," or the settling of old scores.

President of the Screen Actors Guild

Reagan gravitated to the Screen Actors Guild (SAG), which he called a "damned noble organization." The board members set an impressive example. "My education was completed when I walked into the board room," a star-struck Reagan wrote in his autobiography. "I saw it crammed with the famous men of business. . . . I knew then I was beginning to find the rest of me." What he saw in the board room was an array of mostly conservative Republican actors (which included women, his wife among them) dedicated to their own economic interests and those of their fellow actors. Reagan became a self-described "rabid union man." After joining SAG in 1937, he became a board member in 1941. As a SAG board member, he took an active role in opposing and eventually defeating the CSU strike in 1946. He won election as president of the organization in March 1947. The SAG presidency gave him a key position of influence in Hollywood.

Contacts with the FBI

A month after becoming SAG president, three FBI agents approached Reagan at his home to warn against past associations, question him, and ask for his cooperation. A partly censored 156-page FBI file on Reagan released publicly in 1985 states that he and Wyman met with the FBI secretly three times in 1947, when together they named at least six people they suspected of Communist ties.

In his autobiography, Reagan recalls one evening when the FBI visited his home. "We thought someone the Communists hated as much as they hate you might be willing to help us," one agent said. Reagan said he did not want to take part in "Red baiting." The agents then told of conversations about him to which they had been privy. These "opened my eyes to a good many things," Reagan said. Recognizing a moral beacon, he hardened his views and weighed further into the anti-Communist drive.

Reagan, identified in FBI records as informer "T-10," has denied he ever took part in labeling and forcing people out of organizations, an activity called "purging." The FBI file, however, contradicts this, saying that Reagan told the FBI he was on a secret committee of producers and actors "the purpose of which allegedly is to 'purge' the motion-picture industry of Communist Party members."

But Reagan was also critical of the committee, which he felt was unqualified to determine "just who is a commie and who isn't," the FBI file says. Reagan said the best procedure would be to outlaw the Communist Party and then take open legal action against its members. This was the official stand adopted by Hollywood producers.

Testifying in Washington

Later in 1947, Reagan was summoned to appear before the House Un-American Activities Committee (HUAC), which led the drive to rid Hollywood of Communists. In the FBI file, Reagan is quoted as objecting to some of the tactics used by HUAC—in particular, the handling of so-called unfriendly, or suspect, witnesses. He appeared in Washington to testify before the committee on October 25 as a "friendly" witness and gave evidence demonstrating the existence of a Communist conspiracy in the film industry.

Before glaring lights and a row of news cameras, Reagan testified that he knew of a "clique [within the SAG] suspected of more or less following the tactics that we associate with the Communist Party." He maintained, "I do not believe the Communists have ever at any time been able to use the motion-picture industry as a sounding board for their philosophy or ideology." These remarks echoed those of the Hollywood producers anxious to show the approved anti-Communist spirit and claim to have kept Communists out of the industry.

Some of those called to testify before HUAC named names, cheapening themselves as informers. Giving names often ruined reputations, destroyed careers, even triggered suicides. Unfriendly witnesses who refused to give the committee any names landed on blacklists themselves.

Reagan named no one, taking a stand praised as supporting civil liberty. It enabled him to keep his reputation as a "moderate" and make a show of loyalty. But having secretly named names for the FBI later drew criticism and suggestions that Reagan had taken a greater part in the anti-Communist witch hunt than had been acknowledged.

DIVORCE

What energy Reagan had left over from his guild work he devoted to acting. In 1947, when he began a lifelong practice of wearing contact lenses to correct his vision, Reagan filmed a number of unsuccessful movies. One was "Stallion Road," a horse story in which, a critic said, "the human beings don't come off as well as the horses." These flops came just after Warner Brothers, apparently convinced by his prewar film successes that Reagan's career could take off, had given him a seven-year, million-dollar contract.

Reagan's heart was no longer in movies and his personal life was suffering. Jane had long tried to share his interest in the Screen Actors Guild, but could not match his intensity or extreme views. Instead, she put more and more time and effort in her acting, especially after she was nominated for Best Actress of the Year for "The Yearling."

In late November 1947, the Reagans were overheard arguing as they were leaving a Hollywood restaurant. As the parking attendant drove their car up to the building, Jane shouted, "I got along without you before and I certainly can get along without you now!" She got in the car and drove away, leaving Ronnie at the curb.

Missing the Warning Signs

The end came in mid-1948. Jane filed for divorce on the grounds of "extreme mental cruelty." She moved out of the house, taking with her Maureen and Michael, whom they had adopted as a newborn on March 18, 1945. The property

Reagan with Jane Wyman and their children, Maureen, 5½, and Michael, 1. About two years later, work pressures and personal differences would lead to the couple's divorce. (Wisconsin Center for Film and Theater Research.)

was divided up: he got the horses; she got the furniture. Their house was sold.

The divorce hit Reagan hard, taking him by surprise. He said: "I suppose there had been warning signs, if only I hadn't been so busy, but small-town boys grow up thinking only other people get divorced. The plain truth was that such a thing was so far from being imagined by me that I had no resources to call upon."

Years later, Reagan acted as if the divorce had not really happened. He felt that he and Jane had not really been divorced because he had never wanted to end the marriage. "I was divorced in the sense that the decision was made by somebody else," he said 32 years later, just before becoming the first President of the United States to have been divorced.

Middle Age

After his divorce, Reagan worked on a film that was shot on location in England. He spent a couple of months there, dissatisfied with his casting and unimpressed with the country. He returned from this first trip overseas late in 1948, hoping for the stardom that had so far eluded him. He wanted to have fame in roles like those of his he-man, tough guy, strong, self-confident idols: Spencer Tracy, James Stewart, Gary Cooper, and John Wayne.

Reagan renegotiated his contract with Warner Brothers to allow more freedom in choosing the pictures he would be in. But whatever he played — a county prosecutor, a worried father, or a Western marshal — his movies left the public cold. Reagan, at age 39 in 1950, was suffering from the onset of middle age, which ends many an acting career.

Chapter 6
Co-Starring Nancy

The conversation at dinner one night in late 1949 at the home of Dore and Miriam Schary drifted to politics. Reagan made his anti-Communist views plain. The hosts, who considered Red-baiting dangerous, felt a tenseness at the gathering. However, a guest named Nancy Davis, sitting opposite Ronald at the table, listened attentively, smiling in agreement. She had found the man of her dreams.

Nancy had written on a questionnaire for her studio biography that her greatest ambition in life was "to have a successful marriage." That was a goal her own parents had not accomplished. Her mother, actress Edith Luckett, and her father, car salesman Kenneth Robbins, had separated soon after her birth on July 6, 1921.

While her mother performed, the child, named Anne Frances Robbins but always known as Nancy, stayed with relatives in Maryland. She suffered an insecure, unhappy childhood. Her parents were divorced in 1929, after which her mother married Chicago doctor Loyal Davis, a man of extreme conservative views. Nancy formed a daughterly attachment to the doctor, eventually taking his last name as her own.

Nancy attended private schools and Smith College, heading to Hollywood after graduation in a half-hearted search for movie parts. She showed little promise, but a career in films never really was what she wanted.

Ronald and Nancy Reagan on their wedding day, March 4, 1952, with the best man, fellow actor William Holden, and his wife, matron of honor Ardis Holden. (National Archives, Reagan Presidential Material Staff).

It seems likely that Nancy met Ronnie in September 1949 at the Schary's (a guest at the dinner recalled the meeting clearly). She herself, however, dates the first meeting to November, when she contacted Reagan at the Screen Actors Guild. Davis wanted him to help end a mixup between her name and that of a blacklisted actress also named Nancy Davis. Reagan invited her to dinner and they hit it off, talking until two or three in the morning.

Whatever occurred, it seems clear Davis found the man

she wanted. They dated steadily and on March 4, 1952, in a simple church ceremony, began a long, happy marriage.

KNOTTY TV ISSUES

Reagan's attention increasingly focused on the Screen Actors Guild and the new knotty issues raised by television, which by 1950 was reaching five million homes. Reagan, as president of the SAG, dove into negotiations to give actors a share in the profits of movies that were shown on television. He was soon drawn into a major talent agency's scramble to take part in the windfall.

A Suspicious Deal

In 1952, the rapid growth of television led to a move by the country's biggest talent agency, Music Corporation of America, or MCA, to fill the demand for TV shows. The Screen Actors Guild, with Reagan playing a key role, granted MCA privileges that enabled it to dominate the field. This action raised suspicions of a payoff between MCA and the guild which in 1962 attracted an investigation by the U.S. Department of Justice.

Reagan, suspected of accepting a kickback, was called upon to give testimony before a federal grand jury, a body which investigates to determine whether there is enough evidence to prosecute a case. He insisted the deal with MCA was designed to generate employment for actors. The truth of the matter was never fully revealed, for the investigation was dropped when MCA sold off its conflicting business on the court's orders.

Reagan resigned his SAG post in 1952 after five terms in office, giving no reason for his departure. Except for a return to serve a term as guild president during 1959–1960 contract talks, his union career drew to a close.

General Electric Theater

Having made little use of his film-choice options with Warner Brothers and having failed to work to improve his acting ability, Reagan was running out of film offers by 1954. But he had to support his family, make divorce payments, and pay for the 290-acre horse ranch—"Yearling Row"—he had purchased near Los Angeles. He needed cash. In desperation, he served as the master of ceremonies for a second-rate show in Las Vegas.

In the fall, MCA came to the rescue. It convinced the massive General Electric (GE) Corporation to choose Reagan for its community relations campaign and weekly television series, "General Electric Theater." Reagan's voice, his looks, and his bearing conveyed the kind of solid, but not too stodgy, image of reliability the company wanted.

For $125,000 and later $200,000 a year, Reagan hosted and sometimes acted in the Sunday night television dramas. He also made personal appearances before many of GE's more than 700,000 employees in 42 states. Traveling by train (he had long feared and avoided air travel), Reagan toured the nation yearly, shaking hands, giving autographs, and making up to 14 speeches a day.

In the early years of his association with GE, Reagan would talk about America, the need for wholesome values, family, national economic problems, taxes—subjects his audience cared about. Gradually, he became a spokesman for big business. He developed what became known as "The Speech" as his main talk. The company appearances and the TV series helped make Reagan a nationally recognized figure.

Everything Electric

The public and private Reagan became a walking symbol of GE. The company oufitted a house the Reagans built in Los Angeles in 1955 with all GE appliances ("Everything electric except a chair," quipped one report). Nancy, a self-admitted "frustrated interior decorator," furnished it with contemporary couches, tub chairs, and glass coffee tables — much of it red, the Reagans' favorite color. GE advertisements featured this "House of the Future" and the Reagans as an example for consumers of generous use of electricity.

Ronald and Nancy had their own family now. Patricia Ann ("Patti") arrived on October 22, 1952. Ronald Prescott ("Skipper") was born on May 21, 1958.

Nancy fitted well into Ronald's life. He called her "honey" and sometimes "mommie." They held hands in public. She liked being a wife and took an interest in whatever her husband did.

Increasingly, that meant politics. Reagan's participation in politics grew through the 1950s as his film career waned through a series of unmemorable films (he played opposite a monkey in one). By 1950, though still a registered Democrat, he worked for the Republicans. That year he helped win a Senate seat for conservative Republican Congressman Richard Nixon, who used harsh Red-baiting tactics against his opponent. By 1952 Reagan was giving speeches and commencement addresses, and he was formulating stands on political issues he had not made public before.

JUMPING INTO POLITICS

In 1960, Democrat John F. Kennedy ran against Nixon to succeed Republican President Dwight Eisenhower. Kennedy, whose charisma and charm set him apart from the less appealing Nixon, won a narrow victory. The Kennedy presidency had a personal impact on Reagan. In 1962, Kennedy began to enforce antitrust laws in order to prevent over-concentration of big business. MCA was among the first of the Kennedy targets. Shortly after the government started investigating MCA, General Electric, giving 24 hours notice, took its drama series off the air. In his autobiography, Reagan blamed this action on competition with the TV western "Bonanza." Scholars, however, have given other explanations. One of the most likely is that GE feared scandal through Reagan's past association with MCA. Others say "The Speech" was getting too controversial. Reagan, lining up with extreme Republican conservatives called the New Right, now openly attacked Roosevelt's New Deal. This put him outside the mainstream of Republicans. Under Eisenhower, the party had accepted the activist role for the federal government that had been established by Roosevelt.

Laying the Groundwork

Reagan's last link to the Democrats was severed when Nelle died on July 25, 1962. He registered officially as a Republican Party member that year. In 1964, after 52 movies, he made his last film, a made-for-TV thriller. The next year he hosted his last TV program, the "Death Valley Days" series. He gave "The Speech" whenever he could now, attracting the notice of influential California Republicans who began to consider Reagan as a possible candidate for governor of the state.

About this time, Reagan began to work with Richard G. Hubler on his autobiography, *Where's the Rest of Me?*, which was published in 1965. The book has been called "a political campaign waiting to happen." While downplaying personal embarrassments, such as his 1962 change of political parties, it describes Reagan's life as a search for his true calling—and lays the groundwork for his entry into politics.

Chapter 7
Right Man, Right Time

Television screens around the country glowed with the familiar face of Ronald Reagan on the evening of Tuesday, October 27, 1964. To viewers, his reassuring smile brought to mind decades of Reagan's "good guy" movie and TV roles. On this occasion, the 53-year-old actor was appearing at a nationally televised $1,000-a-plate, fund-raising dinner in Los Angeles to boost Republican presidential candidate Barry Goldwater. Reagan read his own speech with his own views of the election issues.

WINNING VOTERS' HEARTS

"You and I have a rendezvous with destiny," said Reagan, looking into the camera. These words recalled the words of President Franklin Roosevelt, from whom the quote was adapted. Reagan encouraged the association, which was comforting to Democrats he hoped to win over. But he blasted much that the Democrats had helped create: high taxes and big government.

In a 27-minute flurry of statistics, stories about a welfare mother, an unfortunate farmer, and a stranded soldier, mixed with a few jokes, Reagan painted a grim picture of the nation under the Democrats. America, he said, was in danger of losing its prosperity, weakening militarily, and yielding freedom to threats from Communism. Reagan declared that preventing these outcomes was of the utmost importance. "We can preserve for our children this, the last best hope of man on earth, or we can sentence them to take the first step into a thousand years of darkness," he said solemnly. "If we fail, at least let our children, and our children's children, say of us we justified our brief moment here. We did all that could be done."

This was a version of "The Speech" Reagan had developed at GE. It echoed and sometimes went beyond the positions of the hard-edged Goldwater, a U.S. Senator from Arizona. Goldwater's harsh delivery helped earn him the label "right-wing extremist," but Reagan's simple, well-timed sentences won voters' hearts. Reagan, always statesmanlike and warm, made viewers feel he was speaking to them through the television.

POLITICAL DEBUT

Reagan's political debut was made possible by the backing of big Republican fund-raisers from California. They wanted to put him on national television not only to win support for Goldwater's presidential candidacy, but also to promote Reagan himself as a politician. However, Goldwater campaign managers, attempting to shed their candidate's right-wing label, opposed the Reagan appearance. They thought his speech was too "emotional" and "unscholarly." Goldwater himself reacted indifferently, but Reagan's backers insisted. They got their way, in part by refusing to release campaign funds in their control for any purpose other than the broadcast.

The speech, entitled "A Time for Choosing," succeeded beyond expectations. Major newspapers ignored Reagan's appearance, but the TV public watched it. It triggered a million-dollar flood of campaign donations into Republican coffers, more than had been raised by any politician's speech up to that time. *Washington Post* columnist David Broder later called it "the most successful national debut since William Jennings Bryan electrified the 1896 Democratic Convention with his 'Cross of Gold' speech," one that "made Reagan a political star overnight." When Goldwater fell to defeat before the massive win for liberal Democrat Lyndon B. Johnson, Reagan inherited from Goldwater the mantle of conservative political leadership in the United States.

He lost no time in making use of his newly gained renown.

THE CITIZEN CANDIDATE

Just months after Reagan's 1964 national television address, a handful of Republican millionaires asked Reagan to be a candidate in the 1966 election for governor of California. They saw him as a Goldwater-type, but with a better image. "Ron was a real leader—he's got credibility. He can get on his feet and influence people," said one extremely wealthy business executive. Reagan accepted the offer. He actually cared little for state politics, having always been concerned about national issues. But the governorship was a steppingstone to the plum Reagan really wanted: the presidency.

The fact that Reagan had never before held public office presented no special problem to his campaign managers, public relations executives Stuart Spencer and Bill Roberts. Reagan would be promoted as a "citizen candidate," an outsider uncontaminated by past practices, a rescuer of the voters from the politicians. This set him apart from Democratic opponent Edmund "Pat" Brown, the state's governor for the past eight years, whose son would succeed Reagan in 1974. Pat Brown looked and sounded like a wheeling-dealing politician.

Developing a Package

Reagan's managers could not so easily overcome Reagan's lack of knowledge about California issues or absence of a political program for the state. Calling in two behavioral scientists to help, Spencer and Roberts secluded Reagan for days to organize his ideas into a saleable package with a simple theme. The theme they settled on was the "Creative Society," where government freed private enterprise, thereby fostering prosperity and reducing big government, welfare, and high taxes.

Because Reagan tended to mix up facts and ideas, the slogan-like points he was to make and the answers he would give were distilled into eight notebooks of five-by-eight cards. These facts and ideas were drilled into Reagan, his managers following him everywhere he went as they reminded him of what to say.

At one news conference, Reagan burst into anger in a debate with a political rival. His managers realized that his sunny nature dimmed when he became tired. They made sure he was rested, scheduling a nap in the afternoon before evening appearances.

During the campaign, Reagan criss-crossed the state by bus and by plane to rally voters. Middle- and working-class people burdened with rising costs and taxes in fast-growing California responded to his appeal. He won the Republican nomination and then the election, with a landslide of nearly a million votes. His opponent, Governor Brown, had underestimated Reagan during the campaign, dismissing him as a political lightweight. Others would make the same mistake later.

A 12:01 A.M. Inauguration

To emphasize the urgency of Reagan's mission, his inauguration (the most expensive swearing-in ceremony in state history) was set for one minute after midnight, January 2, 1967. His team felt they had to make a mark quickly, to earn for Reagan a record of accomplishments for the 1968 presidential race.

This would be no simple task. Reagan had no political experience, no political machine. He had ideas, but no plan to translate them into reality. He knew little about how government functioned. Neither did his staff. "The big question was 'My God, what do we do now?' " said press secretary Lyn Nofziger. The lack of experience would soon show.

Reagan was in for a shock. Due to Brown's delays in raising taxes and his bookkeeping gimmicks, it was discovered only after taking office that the state would soon start running out of money unless taxes went up. Having campaigned against taxes, Reagan was in a bind. What could be done?

At this point, Reagan made his first big mistake. Certain that "there are simple answers—there just are not easy ones," he called for an across-the-board 10 percent cut in spending. This apparently easy solution was suggested by his finance director, who chose it because he did not have enough time to figure out the 1,005-page state budget before the legal deadline.

The approach soon backfired. The cuts affected both well-funded and poorly funded programs equally. The impact on the most needy programs, especially mental health, resulted in such outcries that the government was forced to rush in extra funds. Later, in many areas, it had to give up more than might have been necessary to still fears stirred by the random budget cutting.

People Problems

Reagan had better luck in dealing with student unrest on the Berkeley campus of the University of California and elsewhere. While he sparred with administrators over rising tuition and the costs of education, he railed against student protests, which, in 1969, became particularly violent. Reagan called the National Guard to Berkeley for 17 days, quelling violence that had left one policeman dead. He was shown on television standing up to shouting students, giving him the image of a tough conservative.

Inexperience on the Reagan staff also caused disasters. The government had been staffed hastily, largely through recommendations by a committee of Reagan's millionaire backers. His chief of staff, the most important position in his administration, was among those brought in by this group. Press aide Nofziger, an ex-journalist, suspected the bright young chief of staff of filling posts with friends whose private sexual conduct was not considered acceptable for public servants and set about collecting evidence. He hoped to expel the individuals before the public heard about them.

For Reagan, who had campaigned against "moral decline" in society, this was a potential scandal. When told of the presence of these people in his administration, he exclaimed, "My God, has government failed?" and withdrew into inactivity for two months. The government went leaderless. The suspected staff members lost their jobs, raising suspicions which eventually led to news media exposure and a severe political blow for Reagan.

The problem occurred because Reagan gave out too much authority to other people, allowing staff differences to get out of control. This loose approach to governing set a pattern for later Reagan administrations, with more serious consequences.

More Talker than Thinker

The chief of staff was replaced. Then William Clark and later Edwin Meese were appointed to key posts. They put together an extraordinarily efficient management team (from which Reagan, when he became President, would draw most of his advisors, including Meese and Clark).

Reagan generally exercised little or no leadership in the formation of policy. He endorsed decisions made by his staff and by officials. Disputes among them were settled before they reached the governor. The process was centralized in the Cabinet meeting, which Reagan would attend but did not preside over. His staff would present him with one-page "mini-memos" of no more than four paragraphs each. No matter how complex the issue, this sheet would summarize it and propose a solution. The meeting served to explain decisions to the governor, rather than make them.

Reagan took an active role, however, in what he could do best: winning people to his cause. His public speech-making role put the best face on the government's actions at the same time as it gauged people's reaction to them. He understood how to choose the fact or line or thought that fixed an idea in the public mind. He conveyed it effectively. Because he believed in what he said, people tended to believe him.

But Reagan's administration still had to find money to fund the state. Notwithstanding the 10 percent cuts, taxes had to be raised. By making political deals with the state legislature, trading political favors for votes, the governor's staff won the biggest tax increase in California history (or any other state). The candidate who had been against big spending, political deals, and high taxes now performed one of his greatest selling feats. Claiming the 10 percent tax cut blunder showed that his administration could keep government costs down, he blamed the tax increase on his Democratic predecessor's overspending. When the 1967 tax hike proved unnecessarily high and resulted in surpluses, he then took credit for expert management.

Presidential Fever

The turnabout in California might have served Reagan well in his presidential aspirations were it not for Richard Nixon. Reagan thought he could get the votes claimed by Goldwater in 1964, but Nixon beat him to it. Reagan, campaigning nationally as an unannounced but acknowledged candidate, found that Nixon had already won commitments from key conservatives. The 1968 Republican National Convention in Miami nominated Nixon, who went on to win the election.

The convention proved such an embarrassment for Reagan that he tried to put it behind him quickly, settling back into his role as governor. With Nixon expected to serve as President until 1976, Reagan had no choice but to return to life as governor for the time being. In 1970 he won a second term as governor against assembly speaker Jesse Unruh, a political powerhouse among Democrats in California but a poor campaigner.

During his second term, Reagan made his only attempt to exercise personal political leadership, calling for a cap on taxation with "the taxpayers' bill of rights." The proposal suffered a stunning defeat, and he went back to letting others take the initiative in policy-making.

Welfare reform was the greatest success of Reagan's second term. He charged in 1970 that welfare was causing the government to cut back on other things people needed "to feed this welfare monster." A reform bill his staff worked out with the legislature limited eligibility for public assistance but increased the amount of money paid to welfare recipients.

"On balance," critics later said, the program was improved and welfare roles began to shrink.

In his second term, Reagan's government hummed along smoothly. It had learned from the mistakes of his first years. Negotiations and planning, rather than overspending and influence peddling, became the tools of the administration now. Reagan's management style was working.

THE REAGAN STYLE

Previous California governors lived in a roomy Victorian mansion located conveniently near the Capitol. The Reagans refused to live there, preferring a more modern residence farther from official business. Obliging wealthy friends, including a top MCA executive, helped out by building for the Reagans a contemporary house intended to become the new governor's mansion. However, it was not finished in time for the Reagans to live there (in fact, no governor ever occupied it). While the house was under construction, the Reagans moved into a residence in an isolated, well-to-do section of Sacramento, also bought for them by friends.

Reagan accepted many such personal favors from business friends. While in office he bought and sold hundreds of acres of ranchland through MCA and 20th Century Fox, both of whom benefited from a 1968 law change under Reagan. The land deals made Reagan truly wealthy. In 1974, he bought the 688-acre Rancho Del Cielo, near Santa Barbara, which would one day become his western retreat from the White House.

At Home with the Reagans

Ronald, 56 when he arrived in the state capital, would go home at night for dinner, typically of meat and potatoes. He would spend the evenings in his swimming pool, watching a TV show or a football game. Public life agreed with him.

Nancy kept up their social life among the wealthy circle of friends she had known in Los Angeles, but found the public spotlight could be hard to take. In 1968 an interviewer wrote:

> Nancy Reagan has an interested smile, the smile of someone who grew up in comfort and went to Smith College and has a father who is a distinguished neuro-surgeon and a husband who is the definition of a Nice Guy, the smile of a woman who seems to be playing out some middle-class American woman's daydream, circa 1948.

The interview, mocking what the journalist saw as Nancy's obsession with appearances, upset Nancy. She felt she had been attacked for being pleasant. "Maybe it would have been better if I snarled a bit," she said to another reporter.

However, the interviewer made a point that other interviewers would make: Nancy came off as stiff and shallow. She seemed to have no interests other than her husband. She looked on Ronald with such admiration at ceremonies that reporters dubbed her look as "the gaze." The look, however, was quite sincere; Ronnie, she said, was her hero. "My life began when I got married," Nancy used to say.

The Reagans had a troubled relationship with their children. One of the books the Reagan children wrote in adulthood described Ronald as unkind and Nancy as superficial. According to others, Ronald seemed to have little interest in the children of his first marriage. Home life could not have been easy.

ADDING IT ALL UP

As long as he let the machinery of government work, Reagan's administration turned out solutions to state problems. These solutions, however, often showed little resemblance to what he said in his upbeat speeches. After all his promises, taxes went up. When he left office in 1975, spending was up on education, the poor, and mental hospitals compared to eight years earlier. His administration enacted liberal legislation on abortion (although he later said he regretted it and reversed his position) and welfare.

Reagan would later claim too much for his state administration or even take credit for the opposite of what happened. Despite his claims to have cut big government, he strengthened it, spending more than either of the Browns and doubling the budget. Reagan would boast of his record in his own terms, however, all the way to the White House.

Chapter 8

Kindling an American Dream

At 2:30 A.M. on June 17, 1972, police arrested five burglars at Democratic Party headquarters in the Watergate apartments in Washington, D.C. The arrests helped set off a chain of events that led to the worst political scandal in U.S. history: the Watergate affair. Disclosures of President's Nixon's illegal measures against political opponents forced him to resign in August 1974. Nixon's Vice-President, Gerald Ford, stepped in to complete the term.

The Watergate affair cast a shadow over the entire Republican Party. When President Ford later pardoned Nixon, esteem plummeted again. Americans considered Republicans dishonest, incompetent, and allied with big business. In the fall of 1974, the party lost 46 seats in Congress and four governorships, including California. Its popularity sank to an all-time low.

All this doubly doused Reagan's presidential hopes. Had Nixon survived to complete his second term, by law he could not run again. Reagan would have run as the leading Republican candidate. Now, not only were Republicans out of favor, but Reagan would have to run against a Republican incumbent, Gerald Ford. Taking on the currently serving President might divide the party and weaken the Republican bid for the presidency, but Reagan was determined to run. Ever hopeful, he had begun working toward his goal even before he became an ex-governor.

A BIT TOO BOLD

In his last year in Sacramento, Reagan had regular breakfast meetings with advisors to plan for the presidential election in 1976. After ending his term as governor, he appeared at speaking engagements around the nation, wrote a newspaper column, and read a regular radio commentary—all sounding themes of "The Speech." Campaign managers mapped out strategy: Reagan would take the high ground by making bold, attention-grabbing proposals.

The bold ideas flopped, however. The first one almost destroyed Reagan's campaign. In September 1975, he made a speech on reducing taxes. He proposed a "transfer of authority and resources" from the federal to state levels that would cut federal spending by $90 billion, balance the budget, and give taxpayers an average 23 percent break.

How the transfer would be made was not spelled out, as Stuart Spencer, now working for Gerald Ford, noticed. The idea raised so many questions that it quickly became known as the "$90 billion blunder." Such bright ideas would cause Reagan to lose vital primary elections, in which candidates compete for support within their party.

A Divisive Challenge

By March 1976 the Reagan campaign was heavily in debt and looked like it might collapse. Reagan campaign manager John Sears secretly explored the idea of joining forces with Ford.

Unexpectedly, however, Reagan won the North Carolina primary. In that state he had moved to the right, attacking Ford himself for the "greatest budget deficit in history," cuts in defense spending, and weakness in the dispute over control of the Panama Canal. ("We bought it, we paid for it, it's ours and we aren't going to give it away to some tinhorn dictator," Reagan would say, invariably to a burst of applause.) The patriotic emphasis worked for Reagan, who now portrayed himself as the outsider ready to shake up the "Washington establishment."

The more hard-edged approach was two-edged. While it won a few primaries, polls showed the shift to the right would have cut Reagan off from mainstream voters needed to win a general election. It brought him to the Republican National Convention, but left him short of the support needed to sew up the nomination. Ford won the nomination and went on to lose a close race for President against Democratic candidate Jimmy Carter.

Critics said Reagan's challenge had forced Ford to improve his campaigning. Ford, nevertheless, blamed his defeat in part on Reagan's candidacy. "How can you challenge an incumbent President of your own party and *not* be divisive?" Ford asked.

Economics on a Napkin

As the story goes, University of Southern California economics professor Arthur Laffer was having drinks one day in 1974 with a White House staff member under Ford. Laffer drew a lopsided igloo shape on a napkin to explain a new idea on taxation: supply-side economics. Helped by the interest of a *Wall Street Journal* reporter, this doodle became the basis for an economic fad with enormous consequences for the economy.

New ideas about economics had hurt the Reagan campaign in 1976, but by 1978 Sears was again looking for something aggressive and hopeful for Reagan's 1980 bid for the presidency. He latched onto supply-side economics. Reagan looked on it with caution at first, for the ideas contradicted much that he had said for decades about fiscal responsibility and balanced budgets.

The theory stated that taxes had become so burdensome that they drained the economy rather than strengthened it. Cutting taxes, easing regulations, taking other measures to remove government control, and giving businesses and taxpayers more money would promote business investment and growth. This, in turn, would foster new industrial plants capable of more and cheaper production. Such growth would generate more wealth for everyone – government included. The theory suited opponents of big government like Reagan.

Politically, the idea had appeal, too. Americans were chafing under taxes. Under Carter, the economy was faltering due to inflation, when prices rise too fast, and stagflation, when economic growth stalls and inflation continues. Traditionally, only an economic slump could cure inflation. Because supply-side theories promised to restore the economy painlessly, Reagan accepted them.

Team Troubles

Reagan claimed the front-runner spot among the formidable Republican candidates lined up for a shot at the presidency in 1980. These included George Bush, the man who was to become Reagan's Vice-President and his eventual successor. Reagan's biggest problem stemmed not from his opponents, but from his own campaign managers' infighting over power. Problems had long been brewing on his campaign team that Reagan had failed to deal with.

The problems came to a head at Reagan's home on Thanksgiving 1979, only a few days before he formally announced his presidential intentions. Sears complained about the work of Michael Deaver, a Reagan aide for more than a decade. Reagan, seemingly without question, accepted the accusations and confronted Deaver as the others looked on. Deaver was stunned by the apparent lack of faith in him. He defended himself. Sears, nevertheless, insisted that Deaver had to go.

Seeing that Sears would not compromise, Nancy Reagan spoke up, saying: "Yes, honey, you're going to have to make a choice." Before Reagan could answer, the balding Deaver responded. "No, governor, you don't have to make that choice, I'll resign." Deaver then stalked out. Sears got his way because Reagan let him monopolize power and push out Deaver, whom Reagan liked. Although Reagan resented Sears for the loss, he needed him for the time being.

Iowa Surprise

Sears stayed on and the campaign got off to a shaky start. Reagan bungled questions about federal aid to New York and key legislation to rescue Chrysler Corporation. On national television he appeared not to know who the President of France was. To avoid such blunders, his managers decided that Reagan should travel by airplane in order to keep him away from the news media, but the strategy soon misfired. In Iowa, site of the first primary, Reagan lost to George Bush.

This shocked Reagan into taking action. In New Hampshire, he shed the "imperial candidate" approach and came back to earth, traveling like other candidates on a bus in reach of reporters. He debated other candidates successfully at Manchester, New Hampshire, on February 20, 1980, boosting his place in the polls and probably securing a winning lead.

Taking Charge

Reagan then made a national splash three days later at a Saturday debate in the high school at Nashua, New Hampshire. During some arguing over the rules while on television, Reagan grabbed a microphone and took control. "I paid for this microphone, Mr. Green," Reagan said, mangling the name of Jon Breen, editor of the *Nashua Telegraph*, the sponsor of the debate, but establishing himself in TV viewers' eyes as a firm leader. The statement showed up the top challenger, George Bush, who had refused to pay for the facilities, letting Reagan's campaign pick up the entire bill. That's what Reagan meant when he said he had "paid for the microphone." In comparison with Reagan's righteous fury, the miffed Bush appeared stiff and unbending, an impression he could not later shake off.

In voting the following Tuesday, Reagan took the state with 51 percent of the vote, with Bush and the others dividing up the rest.

While the press focused on his victory, Reagan quietly took the step he had so long avoided to bring harmony to his team. Pressed again by Nancy, he fired the uncompromising Sears and his associates. He brought back Deaver and hired new campaign managers, easing management conflicts. He acted in time.

The drive gained momentum that would carry Reagan all the way to the Republican National Convention in Detroit on July 13. By then, his nomination was secure—only the choice of running mate was in question. With some doubts, Reagan finally settled on Bush, a moderate. The inclusion of Bush aimed to win over the party's left and center, thereby broadening the ticket's appeal to voters.

FROM BLOOPERS TO VICTORY

On a rubble-strewn lot in New York City's South Bronx, Reagan found himself face to face with a shouting crowd. Unemployed and angry, they heckled him before television cameras he had hoped would record an attack on Carter's broken promises. In 1977 Carter had visited the same lot in an impoverished, rundown section of the city vowing to bring homes and jobs. Four years later, nothing had changed.

As Reagan tried to hold his press conference amid the gutted buildings, jeering drowned out his words. "Talk to the people not the press," the residents demanded, but when he talked to them they jeered even more.

Finally, Reagan had had enough, "I can't do a . . . thing for you if I don't get elected," he said. The crowd settled down enough for him to deliver his statement. Again, Reagan's commanding presence saved the day. The evening television news showed an angry but in-charge candidate putting down the crowd in a way that won respect even from the hecklers. In a campaign against Carter's "mediocre leadership," Reagan appeared as a strong leader, averting what could have been disaster.

Bloopers by Both Sides

Reagan bloopers, however, caused trouble. As in his days as a sports announcer, he showed a flair for drama over accuracy. In a speech in Racine, Wisconsin, he told a favorite story of a bomber pilot in World War II who instructed his crew to bail out after the plane was hit. One crew member was too badly wounded to move, so the pilot, finding the crew member in tears, said, "Never mind, son, we'll ride it down together." Reporters noticed that if both men went down together and died, neither would have been around to report these last words. Reagan had probably confused history with a 1944 movie he had once seen.

Other remarks proved damaging, too. Vietnam War opponents lashed out at Reagan's characterization of the conflict as a "noble cause." They thought the war was a gigantic mistake. Pro-China supporters objected to remarks on Taiwan, forcing him to make a retraction. He got in trouble by wrongly linking Carter to the racist Ku Klux Klan. Such remarks began prompting questions about Reagan's own competence.

Carter, who made a few bloopers himself, encouraged the questions, painting his opponent as a simplistic and dangerous right-wing warmonger. He unwisely tried to press the attack on Reagan, but as always, Reagan was able to deflect the assaults. Reagan's age was expected to be his weakness in the campaign. But since 1976, he had stayed so active giving radio broadcasts, writing newspaper columns, and preparing for 1980 that his age (69) never became an issue.

Reagan's gaffes made little difference. Fortunately for him, most came early in the race. As election day neared, another matter came to the forefront in voters' minds: Jimmy Carter.

Turning the Tables

When the candidates met in late October for their one and only face-to-face television debate, the easygoing Reagan sealed his advantage. What stung most were Reagan's sharp replies to Carter's remarks. "There you go again," he said, avoiding a point on health care policies and making Carter look like he was whining about nothing. Viewers rated Reagan the winner, but the debate probably had little to do with the election outcome.

Throughout the campaign, Reagan had urged voters to think about the losses suffered under Carter. Abroad, the nation was suffering humiliation at the hands of Iran. Months before, on November 4, 1979, extremists had overrun the U.S.

embassy in Teheran, the Iranian capital, and were still holding 52 staff members hostage. Carter seemed helpless to negotiate an end to the months of captivity.

What hurt Carter most was the domestic economy. Over and over on the campaign trail Reagan had asked voters, "Are you better off now than you were four years ago?" Double-digit inflation had cut into pocket books; the people blamed Carter. On November 7, 1980, Reagan triumphed, winning 43,904,153 votes, or 50.7 percent, against Carter's 35,483,883, or 41.0 percent, with the rest going to three minor candidates.

Polls of voters leaving voting places indicated that more than voting for Reagan, the people had rejected Carter. Even so, Reagan interpreted the vote as a "mandate" (an authorization to act) from the voters for his political and economic programs.

ERA OF RENEWAL

The man who would be the 40th President of the United States, the oldest ever to take office, stood before the nation on the steps of the west side of the Capitol. On this bright and sunny January 20, 1981, before the monuments of Washington, the handsome six-foot-one inch, 185-pound Ronald Reagan, dressed in a dark suit, raised his right hand and took the oath of office. Nancy stood at his side. The outgoing President, Jimmy Carter, looked on a few steps away as millions watched the spectacle on television and from the audience.

In his address to the nation, Reagan declared the control of inflation as a first priority. He promised to accomplish this by curbing "the size and influence of the federal government," cutting government spending, and lightening "our punitive tax burden." In a reference to the troubles that had shaken American self-confidence, he waxed optimistic,

President and Mrs. Reagan on a plane at Andrews Air Force base welcome the U.S. hostages released after 444 days of captivity in Iran. (The White House.)

saying, "We are not, as some would have us believe, doomed to inevitable decline." He promised to launch an "era of national renewal," including a buildup of American military strength. He urged Americans to share his outlook, to believe in themselves and in heroism.

Minutes after the inaugural, Iran freed the U.S. hostages, ending their 444 days of captivity. The release was arranged by Carter, but was seen as a symbol of the new Reagan era.

Chapter 9

Reaganomics

Early one afternoon, just over two months into his presidency, Reagan emerged from the Washington Hilton Hotel after speaking at a labor union meeting. He walked toward a waiting limousine, waving his right hand to a group of reporters and photographers standing in a roped-off area nearby. One tried to ask a question, calling out, "Mr. President, Mr. President."

Suddenly, 25-year-old drifter John W. Hinckley, who had been standing among the journalists, dropped into a crouch. Holding a .22-caliber handgun in a two-handed grip and with arms extended, he opened fire.

Within seconds, two shots, and then four more, rang out with a deceptively innocent popping sound. At the first shot, a Secret Service guard reached for the President, pushing him hard through the open back door and onto the floor of the armored limousine.

"Take off!" the guard shouted to the driver. "Just take off!"

As the car screeched away, a policeman, a second protective agent, and Reagan's press secretary, James Brady, lay wounded on the sidewalk. Security men disarmed the mentally disturbed attacker.

Inside the limousine, Reagan felt a pain in his side and coughed up blood. The driver raced to the hospital. Doctors found a bullet had punctured his lung and come to a stop just an inch from his heart. As they prepared Reagan for immediate surgery, Nancy arrived. "Honey, I forgot to duck," said her husband. As he was being wheeled into the operating room, Reagan said to the surgeons, "I hope you're all Republicans." A doctor answered, "Today, everyone's a Republican."

COOL UNDER FIRE

Due to prompt medical treatment, the bullet wound never threatened Reagan's life. Twelve days after the March 30, 1981, assassination attempt, he walked out of the hospital, telling reporters he felt "great." The shooting aroused a surge of support for Reagan, partly because, as Presidents are supposed to be, he was cool under fire. A month later, he gave a speech to a joint session of Congress that was a triumphant return to the helm of the nation.

Whether or not Reagan's landslide victory over Jimmy Carter had provided a mandate for his policies, as he claimed, soon became a question of only academic interest. After the shooting, his popularity rose to an all-time peak. The new President gathered the support he needed to carry out what was called the "Reagan Revolution."

Supply-Side Economics

Reagan's administration called first for reductions in taxes and government spending. He promised at the same time to reduce deficits, (spending more money than is taken in through taxes and other income). He also promised to balance the federal budget by 1984.

Many economists believed this "supply-side economics" was based more on wishful thinking than on reality, but Congress could not resist. By trading with special interests, Reagan won congressional approval for increased defense spending and simultaneous cutbacks on services ranging from school lunch programs and college benefits to welfare and medical aid for the poor. Congress also approved a three-year, 25 percent rollback of individual and business income taxes.

For a while, the "Reagan Revolution" continued. In August, he defeated a nationwide strike by 11,800 air-traffic controllers, creating enemies among labor while winning points in the fight against rising wages, which contributed to inflation. But within months, budget chief David Stockman revealed that the supply-side strategy had caused a reduction in government revenue that could not be offset by spending cuts or economic growth. The government was expected to go badly into the red. Further cuts were made, but they could not cover the imbalance.

Though the shortfall grew, Reagan refused to raise taxes and refused to impose limits on defense spending. He once told Stockman, "Defense is not a budget issue. You spend what you need." Stockman failed to convince the President that billions of dollars in duplication and waste could be trimmed from defense costs. Money spent on weapons resulted in the biggest peacetime military buildup in U.S. history.

Evaporating Goodwill

Soon chants of "we told you so" from economists grew to a deafening pitch. Worried banks kept interest rates high, making it hard for businesses to borrow money; the stock market nose-dived. As a result, five months into Reagan's term, the economy went into a recession (a slowdown) in late 1981 that would last through most of 1982.

The goodwill that Reagan had built up in the spring following the assassination attempt quickly evaporated. Though inflation and interest rates declined, polls showed that by late 1982 Reagan's approval ratings were slipping toward an all-time low. In congressional elections that November, the Republicans lost 26 seats in the House, a shift that translated into greater congressional resistance to Reagan's policies.

The unemployment rate in 1982 shot up to 10.7 percent, the highest since the Depression. More banks failed than at any time since 1940. Record business bankruptcies and farm foreclosures were occurring. Even some Reagan staff members began to admit what George Bush had said while campaigning against Reagan in the Republican primaries: supply-side theories were "voodoo economics." Stockman called the 1982 recession "an utter, mind-numbing catastrophe." The disaster forced Reagan to raise some taxes.

A Costly Experiment

From the end of 1982, the economy began a slow recovery. Inflation was controlled, dropping to 4.1 percent in 1983, and the cost of borrowing money—interest rates—declined by about one-half. These changes are considered among the triumphs of Reagan's first term—even though a reduction in inflation is the usual result of a recession. But the cost of the recession and the lingering effects in the rebound that followed were staggering.

The recession cost the average person $1,000 in lost income and over $3,000 for the average family, with the lower half of society losing four to five times as much as the upper half. Reagan's economic policies, dubbed "Reaganomics," weakened the economy so much that Americans were less well off financially at the end of Reagan's first term than they had been at the end of four years under Carter.

Instead of reducing government spending, Reagan had increased overall federal expenditures during his first term while taking in less revenue. Instead of balancing the budget, he ended up adding to the deficit and greatly increasing the national debt (the amount of money the government must borrow to pay its bills when it spends more than it takes in). The government accumulated as much debt in the first four years of the Reagan administration as had been accumulated to date in U.S. history.

The biggest benefactor of all the spending was the military. Much of the money was spent well, but much of it also went into such questionable projects as the Strategic Defense Initiative, the so-called "Star Wars." Reagan launched the plan in 1983, saying it could protect the country from nuclear attack with an impenetrable space-based anti-missile shield—a claim that many scientists doubted. Reagan, nevertheless, pushed the untested dream as a solution to the arms race between the United States and the Soviet Union. However, after Reagan left office in 1988, the defense program, including the Star Wars project, was shifted dramatically toward less costly military targets.

FOREIGN AFFAIRS

Reagan never missed a chance to talk tough about America in the bigger world. The sharpest words he saved for the Russians. In March 1983, he called the Soviet Union the "evil empire" and said it would lie, cheat, steal, and commit any crime to achieve its ends. This established his anti-Communist credentials, but soured relations with Moscow and bogged down nuclear disarmament talks. Reagan became the first President since Truman to go four years without holding a summit meeting with the Soviets.

In most areas, Reagan's foreign policies won few laurels for his administration. In the Middle East and Central America, his envoys made little headway in settling regional quarrels. Popular opposition to regimes in the Philippines, Argentina, Haiti, and South Africa forced Reagan to lessen his support of these governments, all of which had bad human rights records. His backing of anti-government Nicaraguan rebels, called "Contras," won support from some quarters in the United States, but ended up bringing little change in Nicaragua.

Sending American Marines on a Middle East peacekeeping mission to Lebanon in October 1983 ended in tragedy. A terrorist drove a truck loaded with explosives into the Marine barracks, killing 241 of them. The attack, which was in retaliation for an ill-considered U.S. policy of shelling rebel Moslem villages in support of the Lebanese government, marked Reagan's greatest foreign policy disaster.

A Small Victory

But just two days after the deaths of the Marines in Lebanon, Reagan scored one of his first term's few foreign policy achievements: the invasion of Grenada. American troops took the tiny Caribbean island from a leftist government that had just come to power by force. A democracy was re-established on the island.

The move received mixed international reaction. Some Caribbean governments expressed gratitude for the action, saying it showed that the United States would not tolerate Communist expansion in the area. But many nations saw it as unwarranted interference in another country's affairs. The Reagan administration justified the invasion by saying that Grenada's leaders were pawns of the region's Communist nations, such as Cuba. Evidence for this later proved flimsy.

Grenada was not much of a victory. The U.S. forces could hardly have failed, enjoying as they did a ten-to-one advantage in men, control of the air, and superior artillery power. The exclusion of reporters from the scene helped suppress the embarrassing fact that two-thirds of the U.S. casualties were caused by accidents or by wild fire from other American soldiers. Yet the military, apparently trying to put a good face on its action, pinned more medals on its soldiers than there had been enemy troops.

REVIVING THE SPIRIT

Grenada, nevertheless, served a greater purpose for the Reagan presidency. It helped Reagan restore Americans' faith in themselves. After suffering humiliation and defeat in Vietnam and Iran, after the troubled presidencies of Johnson, Nixon, Ford, and Carter, after Watergate, after Reagan's own failure in Lebanon, America suffered from considerable self-doubt. Many people were wondering what had happened to the greatness of America.

Grenada provided a bit of reassurance to Americans that theirs was still a strong country. Reagan encouraged the feeling. In all his speeches, before and after Grenada, he promoted patriotism, traditional values, and a sense of national destiny. He acted as a father figure, a cheerleader, as well as commander of America's armed forces. He brought the aura of strong leadership to the Oval Office (the President's office in the White House). People responded to his ideals and outlook, looking again to the President for leadership. Grenada was possibly Reagan's "most significant accomplishment," *Newsweek* magazine said at the end of the first term.

Chapter 10

The Teflon Factor

Why was Reagan so well liked? ". . . Immunity from all the usual laws of politics – the Teflon factor – is the ultimate mystery of Ronald Reagan's success," concluded *Newsweek* in a 1984 roundup on the President.

A political opponent had coined the description of Reagan as a "Teflon" President out of frustration. Like Teflon, which is a coating on frying pans that prevents food from sticking, Reagan seemed to have an immunity to his opponent's attacks. However, what he really had was not an immunity, but his own attractiveness – and a staff exceptionally well attuned to shaping his public image.

MASTERFUL PUBLIC RELATIONS

If you turned on the television any day during the Reagan years, chances were good that you would soon see and hear Ronald Reagan. He might have been standing on the White House steps greeting a foreign dignitary like Egyptian President Anwar Sadat. It he were abroad, the cameras might have captured a two-minute spot of the American leader reviewing a bearskin-hatted British honor guard or wearing a flak jacket and standing behind sandbags while snappily saluting battle-ready U.S. troops on the Korean Peninsula.

Wherever he might have appeared, Reagan would probably look happy, confident, and slightly regal. The picture would attract the eye and the action perk interest. That it might recall a movie scene would be no coincidence. Reagan's day was as carefully planned and scheduled as the shooting of an epic.

"Photo opportunities" and ceremonies at the White House were arranged daily in which "every moment . . . was scheduled, every word was scripted, every place where Reagan was expected to stand was chalked with toe marks," a White House insider wrote. Color-coded cue cards told him what to do, where to face, whom to shake hands with, what statements, banter, and greetings to use.

Building an Image

Behind the scenes, the public relations staff went to extraordinary ends to make sure people liked what they saw and heard of Reagan. Though the President was often called "The Great Communicator," press conferences, where he might face tough questions from journalists and bungle the answers, occurred several months apart.

Reagan's image, especially on television, had top priority in his administration. Not only would the staff manage public appearances, but "the innermost secrets of the Administration" would be leaked to curry favor among journalists, said one member of Reagan's Cabinet. Results of polls and word-by-word electronic measurement of audience reaction to his speeches provided a golden standard of success that was reported to the President monthly. The amount of energy devoted to public relations by White House staff members amazed some officials.

The operation was "a system which had at its heart an evidently irresistible desire to save the President's popularity even if this meant undermining the President's policies," said Alexander Haig, the first secretary of state in the Reagan Cabinet. Reagan advisors made certain every presidential action had a positive effect on the public—even if it meant changing a policy to enhance the play it might receive on the news. The news media, themselves a bit dazzled by Reagan's act, eased off the close scrutiny that is usually given to Presidents.

MANAGEMENT STYLE

Books written by Cabinet officials and members of Reagan's staff after leaving the administration paint a picture of a President who took his underlings' advice, usually without question. He left policy-setting and all the details of governing, including the appointing of his own aides and officials, almost completely to others.

The staff energetically kept up appearances, but often had no clear idea as to what the President wanted. Reagan "trusted his lieutenants [subordinates] to act on his intentions rather than on his spoken instructions," said Donald Regan, who parted from Reagan bitterly angry after serving as secretary of the treasury and later as White House chief of staff.

Regan may have been grinding a personal axe, but his view is not much different from that of Martin Anderson, a first-term aide who left the White House on good terms. According to Anderson, Reagan's attitude left him open to certain dangers "if any of his personal staff chooses to abuse his or her position and deliberately withhold key information, Reagan is helpless—and disaster can strike." In his second term, the practice would lead to Reagan's lowest moment: the Iran-Contra affair.

The Jellybean Cabinet

Reagan relied on close subordinates to such a great extent that even Cabinet appointees had difficulty getting to see him. Alexander Haig, who had known Reagan casually before his appointment as secretary of state, hoped to become better acquainted with Reagan in Washington. However, he was never allowed into the inner circle—made up of Edwin Meese, Michael Deaver, and James A. Baker—and spent a rather frustrating time in office.

These aides, breaking with tradition, attended Cabinet meetings, and Meese often led the meetings while the President passed a jar of jellybeans around the table. Reagan said little at the meetings. Instead, he would doodle on his presidential notepad and sometimes nodded off. When Haig brought policy ideas to the White House, the President's advisors often worked to undermine them. Haig never figured out exactly who was making decisions.

To Haig, the White House was "as mysterious as a ghost ship; you heard the creak of the rigging and groan of the timbers, and sometimes even glimpsed crew on deck," he wrote. "But which of the crew had the helm? . . . It was impossible to know for sure."

Unable to find out what the President wanted or expected in foreign policy, Haig found himself in a tug-of-war with the advisors, who would make statements from the White House that contradicted his own. The temperamental Haig was forced to resign on June 25, 1982, to give way to a less abrasive successor, George Shultz, a corporation executive who would hold the position of secretary of state through Reagan's second term.

Changing of Cabinet members and staff occurred often during Reagan's administration. Friction with the White House was but one of the reasons.

LIGHTNING ROD PERSONALITIES

Certain Cabinet members attracted—by design of the White House image makers—the controversy that Reagan shed. On environmental issues, it was Secretary of the Interior James G. Watt, a conservative advocate of greater use of public lands and resources for economic development. He led the drive to change the nation's environmental laws. "Watt did become a lightning rod, and he knew that when he came in. It was a conscious policy in terms of shaping the news," said David Gergen, a Reagan public relations official. Watt, who ended up producing more bad feelings than change, was forced to resign in spring 1983. His policies attracted a bit too much lightning.

In other cases, staff changeovers reflected lax standards of conduct. By the end of his eight years as President, more than 100 senior Reagan officials had been indicted, forced to resign, or accused of illegal or unethical conduct. In his second term, the Iran-Contra affair would lead to top-level criminal prosecutions of White House aides who tried to cover up activities by shredding documents and lying to Congress. And an investigation in 1989 exposed political favoritism in the Department of Housing and Urban Development during Reagan's administration.

All of these improper activities were seen as related to Reagan's own attitudes. Comments he made suggested he was not much concerned when his officials landed in trouble. To a scholar of White House behavior, Reagan seemed "astonishingly unconcerned about displaying a keen sense of propriety." Proper behavior, however, was not always measured by legal or ethical standards. Changeovers sometimes followed when an official fell short on the measuring stick used by Nancy Reagan.

Nancy the Worrier

"At times, Ronald Reagan has been very much a puzzle to me," wrote Michael Deaver, one of the President's aides. "I had never known anyone so unable to deal with close personal conflict. When problems related to the family or office personnel arose, Nancy carried the load." She was above all the one in whom Reagan confided. She took on herself the dirty work he shunned.

Nancy constantly saw betrayals and fretted over potential problems. She complained to Deaver about bad press, this or that senator, or what she thought was an over-busy schedule undermining Ronald's health. She accused aides of "brutalizing" the President with too many facts or making him shake too many hands. When she believed Ronald needed protection, she acted, engineering ousters such as those of Watt, Secretary of Labor Raymond Donovan, and, in the second term, allegedly, Donald Regan. Nancy, however, has played down her role in White House power struggles.

Deaver, who found the First Lady "very intense, sometimes brittle in her manner" but more approachable than her husband, thinks Nancy had a moderating influence on Reagan's policies. She was not really political. Her main concern was Ronald's well-being and the high-society life she loved.

An Extravagant Life-Style

In the fishbowl of life at the White House, Nancy's life-style drew criticism. The public, reeling from budget cuts and reductions of social welfare in 1981, reacted angrily to Nancy's spending of $800,000 raised from private donations to redecorate the White House living quarters. The anger burst out again when it was revealed that the First Lady accepted free clothes, including a $10,000 dress worn at an inaugural ball, from a high-fashion designer. Critics said Nancy's launch of a personal anti-drug campaign in early 1982 was intended to draw attention away from her public image as the extravagant wife of a rich man.

Another flap came in 1988, when Donald Regan revealed that "virtually every major move and decision the Reagans made" had to be approved in advance by an astrologer. Nancy later said she had conducted phone consultations with a San Francisco astrologer since 1981. The astrologer said her advice influenced the timing of the President's speeches, landings of Air Force One (the President's plane), and Reagan's eventual change of heart about the Soviet Union. Reagan, though long reported to be superstitious, denied that he had ever acted on the basis of astrology.

A PLEASANT HOME

Protecting Ronald was not just Nancy's priority. Much of the White House routine focused on giving Reagan the life-style he desired. A regular and predictable schedule was one of these requirements. As a result, Donald Regan said, the President's day was governed by a sort of "shooting script" that Reagan followed religiously, arriving punctually and rarely letting a conversation run over the allotted time. Reagan cooperated with "practically superhuman good nature" to the schedule set out for him, Regan wrote.

A Typical Day

In a typical day for the President, a wake-up call from the White House operator roused Ronald and Nancy from their king-sized bed at 7:30 A.M. He dressed and, while at breakfast, read a news summary compiled by the White House staff. He also read some newspapers, looking first at the comics and certain conservative columnists. He went to the Oval Office at nine sharp, where Meese, Baker, and Deaver, having already held meetings, might be waiting to discuss the coming day with the President.

Before settling down to work, Reagan often fed the squirrels on the terrace outside the Oval Office. At 9:30 the National Security Council officer came in to brief the President on world affairs. (Carter, who was criticized as a workaholic, woke at 6:00 A.M. daily to prepare for a presidential briefing on national security at 7:30 A.M. Reagan, who wanted to sleep later, had the briefing moved to 9:30 A.M.) From 10:00 to 11:00, Reagan read or did correspondence. Often he wrote in longhand to citizens, responding to "moving stories" selected for him from letters that arrived at a rate of up to 20,000 a day—more than for any other President.

At noon, Reagan ate a light lunch, after which he followed the schedule of events for the day, drawing a line through each completed activity. He left the Oval Office for the residential area of the White House at four or five in the afternoon, usually taking a folder of papers to work on in the evening.

When no state dinner was planned, Reagan spent the evenings with Nancy. Before dinner at 6:00 P.M., he exercised by lifting weights. He and Nancy would go to bed by 10:30 or 11:00. The next day, Reagan would arrive at the Oval Office with all his work done, handing the papers over to his personal secretary on the way in.

It was, by presidential standards, a rather leisurely existence. Weekends were spent at Camp David, the presidential retreat in Maryland. The Reagans also spent a record amount of time on vacation.

Reagan's White House advisors — (from left to right) Michael Deaver, James Baker, and Edwin Meese — at the peak of their influence and power on April 24, 1981. (National Archives, Reagan Presidential Material Staff.)

MORNING IN AMERICA

Reagan campaigned for re-election in 1984 under the banner of "Leadership That's Working." His speeches and "It's Morning in America" advertisements focused on simple positive messages, celebrations of patriotism, opportunity, and hope. The "U.S. was never meant to be a second best nation," he said. Under his presidency, said the candidate, the nation had become a "giant economically and militarily." Reagan's unique chemistry with voters inspired pride and confidence.

The President's plans for his second term consisted primarily of continuing the policies of his first term. He had achievements to build on. The military revival was well on its way. The federal government was cutting back on taxation and regulation of business. Big government and the welfare state were under attack. States were taking on responsibilities that Washington had once handled. Presidential appointees to the federal judicial system moved the courts into more conservative positions. Reagan was changing the shape of the nation.

With vitality slowly returning the the economy, Reagan declared that the recovery stemmed from the success of supply-side economics. In truth, however, the recovery was largely due to the bitter medicine of a recession and to a timely drop in international oil prices. Federal deficits continued to increase. But Reagan, disputing experts, including David Stockman, his budget chief, believed the nation would outgrow the problem. His faith in himself and the future of America was unsinkable.

"Just an Innocent Jest"

As in earlier political races, Reagan was wont to put his foot in his mouth once in a while. At one point during the presidential campaign of 1984, he joked into a live microphone, "My fellow Americans, I am pleased to tell you that I've signed legislation that will outlaw Russia forever. We begin bombing in five minutes." Aides said this was just an innocent jest made to test the microphone. Even so, the remark made Reagan look trigger-happy and provoked a sharp international rebuke. After that, Reagan's campaign managers kept him far from reporters throughout the race to avoid other embarrassing, off-the-cuff remarks.

Reagan's Democratic opponent, former Carter Vice-President Walter F. Mondale, was no match for the President before the television cameras. Mondale attacked Reagan's policies, but he could not get Americans interested in what he was saying. Then, when Mondale took the politically unwise step of announcing he would raise taxes, he lost even more voters.

Mondale, who was 56 years old, hoped Reagan's age might become an issue. But in the second of two debates in October, Reagan, now 73 years old, took the public's mind off his age with a quip. "I will not make age an issue of this campaign," Reagan said when asked about age. "I am not going to exploit for political purposes my opponent's youth and political inexperience." The humorous remark swept away the only major concern voters had about Reagan. He had faltered in the first debate, but came out strong from the second.

49 Out of 50

On election day, November 6, 1984, Ronald Reagan swept 49 of the 50 states. Democrats by the millions, especially the young and blue-collar ethnic voters, crossed over party lines to vote for Reagan: blacks, Jewish men, Hispanics, and those earning under $12,500 a year were the only groups that did not support him strongly. The win broke all presidential voting records since Roosevelt's victory in 1936.

Television: Worth More than 1,000 Words

The public saw President Carter on TV stumble while jogging. But people never saw Reagan in less than an inspiring scene. His staff, with the President's cooperation, took great pains to orchestrate TV coverage. More so than for any previous President, the Reagan White House made use of the tendency of people to react to government actions on the basis of what they see on TV.

Television is such a powerful medium that it can amplify or overwhelm negative news. The White House, under Michael Deaver and others, worked hard to achieve the latter. They understood a "simple truism about television: the eye always predominates over the ear when there is a fundamental clash between the two," said Sam Donaldson, a White House reporter for the American Broadcasting Company.

Reagan's staff used this truism to help tide over low moments in his presidency. When Reagan's Lebanon policy failed, leading to a humiliating withdrawal of U.S. Marines from that country, he showed up on television at his hometown speaking to a carefully screened crowd of Republicans. The TV reporter's words heard over the pictures might recount the failure, but, "the *pictures* are of your old friend and mine, Ronald Reagan, before a crowd of cheering people . . . and it's what people see that counts," said Donaldson.

Television reporters, pressed for time and competing with other channels to produce the most attractive, eye-catching stories, fell into the White House trap. They often ended up, unintentionally, being used to promote the President's popularity.

This kind of manipulation of television and other news media by the White House came at a cost. The presidency was strengthened, but the public was less well informed, thereby weakening the processes of democracy.

After watching nearly three decades of weak or failed presidencies, Reagan believed his own presidency was in a position of full strength at the start of his second term in 1985. Political commentators proclaimed that the job of the nation's chief executive might finally be revived, that it could become popular and effective once again. Republicans believed they were poised to enter a new era of political leadership. If there were any doubts of the Reagan mandate in 1980, his overwhelming re-election in 1984 seemed to sweep them away.

Chapter 11

The Undoing of the President

Reagan returned to the White House from Camp David, cutting his weekend short. He went directly to the secret Situation Room in the basement and took his place at the conference table. Aides sat in their places for a special meeting of the National Security Council, the highest crisis management body in the federal government. Reagan unfolded a letter to read aloud. It was a plea from passengers on board a plane hijacked to Beirut, Lebanon.

AN IMPRESSIONABLE AND SENTIMENTAL MAN

At that moment on Sunday, June 16, 1985, the passengers and crew of TWA flight 847 sat in the airplane on the darkened Beirut airport runway. Two days before, armed Moslem extremists had hijacked the jet while it was en route from Cairo to Rome and were pressing authorities to meet a list of demands, especially the release of some 700 Lebanese held in an Israeli prison. They threatened to kill their 39 American captives unless the demands were met. To show they meant business, the extremists murdered one passenger, a 23-year-old U.S. Navy diver, shoving his body out the door of the airplane onto the runway.

"We implore you not to take any direct military action on our behalf," said the letter Reagan read to his advisors. "Please negotiate quickly our immediate release by convincing the Israelis to release 700 Lebanese prisoners as requested. Now."

Reagan looked up and asked what he needed to do to free the Americans. Although U.S. warships floated offshore from Lebanon, any military action might endanger the hostages. Reagan wondered whether it might be possible to pressure Israel into releasing the prisoners to win the Americans' freedom. But Secretary of State George Shultz responded sternly, saying a trade like that would amount to giving in to the terrorists, a policy Reagan had often condemned publicly.

The meeting ended inconclusively. National Security Advisor Robert "Bud" McFarlane and other top advisors left, however, with an insight into the President's reaction. Reagan's impulse to read aloud the letter written under extreme duress by the hostages suggested he was an impressionable and sentimental man.

This was a side of the President that advisors with a longer acquaintance with him had recognized earlier. "He always went for hard luck stories. He sees the plight of real people before anything else," said first-term budget director David Stockman. "Despite his right-wing image, his ideology and philosophy always take a back seat when he learns that some individual human being might be hurt." This posed a danger. Left to his own good intentions, Reagan might confuse individual interest and national goals.

A LIVING NIGHTMARE

Soon after Reagan took office for his second term, he vowed, "Let terrorists beware: when the rules of international behavior are violated, our policy will be one of swift and effective retribution." The words were meant to mark his get-tough attitude with terrorists like those who took hostages at the U.S. embassy in Teheran in November 1979. Carter's "foreign policy helped create the entire situation that made their kidnap possible," Reagan had said when running against Carter in 1980. "I think the fact that they've been there [so] long is a humiliation and disgrace."

Other American Hostages

Now, in 1985, Reagan looked as helpless as Carter did in 1979. Little could be done but patiently negotiate for the TWA hostages. Their well-televised ordeal drew attention to the plight of seven other Americans being held hostage in Lebanon by extremists: a missionary, a news service reporter, four educators, and a man later acknowledged to be CIA station chief in Beirut. These men had chosen to work in Lebanon despite warnings of danger, but their families were no less anguished by their captivity, dating from 1984 in some cases.

Family members of the seven hostages met Reagan at a school near Chicago at this time. They expressed deep anger about how little the U.S. government was doing to free their loved ones. The anger, directed at Reagan himself, made an "indelible impression," an aide recalled.

Waning Popularity

The TWA hostages were finally freed on June 30, when—though Washington vowed it had not struck a deal—Israel began to release the Lebanese prisoners. The hijacked Americans returned home with great fanfare, but Reagan could not forget the seven other hostages still in Lebanon. He committed himself to freeing them, asking day after day of his advisors, "Anything new?"

Reagan had other reasons for anxiety. In the spring of 1985, due to inept planning, he had suffered a major embarrassment. On a trip to West Germany, he had made a ceremonial visit at the Bitburg cemetery, where Nazi troops who had operated World War II death camps were buried. This prompted protests from war veterans and Jewish groups, sending the President's popularity polls into a nose dive. He sorely needed a comeback.

A Bitter Feud

Secretary of State George Shultz was at wit's end. Defense Secretary Caspar "Cap" Weinberger opposed Shultz's moderate views on virtually every issue. Bitter fighting between Shultz and the more conservative Weinberger had raged too long. In late 1984, with the second term about to begin, Shultz went to Reagan to ask him to sort things out once and for all.

"The two of us are unable to work congenially [in a friendly way]," Shultz said. "You should take one or the other."

This amounted to a demand that the President ask Weinberger to resign, or else Shultz would offer his resignation.

"George," the President said, "I'll think about it. But I definitely want you on my team. Make no mistake about that."

Reagan made no decision, ignoring the problem, as he did most staff conflicts. This allowed feuding to rage and led sometimes to uncoordinated or competing policies from the various departments of the executive branch of the federal government.

In the first term, longtime advisors used administrative checks and balances to moderate Reagan's style of management. By the second term, Deaver had gone to work as a lobbyist (one who tries to influence legislators), Meese became attorney general, Baker took over as secretary of the treasury. "There was no one left who understood Reagan," said William P. Clark, the first-term National Security Advisor. Donald Regan, Deaver's replacement as the new chief of the White House staff, was less familiar with Reagan's weaknesses and just "let Reagan be Reagan." In other words, Regan did not understand the moderating role Reagan's advisors had always played. Instead, he allowed Reagan's conservative political instincts and casual oversight of government to reign. This helped cause a dangerous breakdown in the administrative process.

ARMS FOR HOSTAGES

The Iran-Contra affair was born just days after the TWA hostages returned home. At a meeting on July 3, 1985, Reagan pressed his staff to get the other hostages out of Lebanon. National Security Advisor Bud McFarlane took the command to heart.

The solution McFarlane found involved Iran. He proposed an opening to "moderates" he believed existed within the radical Iranian regime. This opening would include a trade of arms for Iranian help in freeing the American hostages still being held in Lebanon. Iran could influence the kidnappers in Lebanon to release the hostages. Although Iran was a sworn enemy of the United States, it would accept the offer because it badly needed U.S. arms to fight a war it was waging against neighboring Iraq. McFarlane thought there could be a way to get around an embargo on trade with Iran that had been imposed by Congress after Iran had held 52 Americans hostage in the U.S. embassy for 444 days.

Opposition to Plan

Shultz and Weinberger, who were usually policy rivals, united in opposition to McFarlane's proposal. "This would undercut everything we were going to do in the Mideast," Weinberger said heatedly at a meeting in August. At the same gathering, Shultz called the proposal "a very bad idea." He was willing to explore new ties to Iran, but "as far as arms sales are concerned, it's a mistake," he said. Both Shultz and Weinberger feared the United States would be undercutting its policy of refusing to deal with terrorists, a policy Shultz was pushing allies hard to observe.

But Reagan, who wanted desperately to free the hostages, approved of the deal. McFarlane, and later his successor, John M. Poindexter, conducted five secret exchanges of arms with Iran, winning freedom for three hostages in deals that involved shady international arms merchants, numbered Swiss bank accounts, and Israeli cooperation. In one trade, McFarlane led a delegation to Teheran disguised as an Irish airline crew member and carrying suicide pills in case he was detected.

Few in the government, not even Shultz and Weinberger, knew until much later that the arms-for-hostages proposal was actually carried out. As for Reagan, he may not have fully realized at the time how the effort became entangled in questionable activities.

Surgery and Power

On July 13, 1985, Reagan transferred all of his presidential powers to Vice-President George Bush and underwent surgery at a Washington hospital for cancer of the colon. Doctors said the operation, in which a section of his intestines was removed, posed no threat to Reagan's life. He took back his powers within a matter of hours after the operation, but spent the next few months recovering. Nancy insisted that aides lighten the President's work load in order to protect his health.

As a result, less information than ever before flowed to the Oval Office. Decision making shifted even more to aides, who, led by chief of staff Donald Regan, kept the President more isolated even after his recovery. Within months, Regan would force McFarlane out as National Security Advisor, removing one of the few balancing forces in the White House and closing off a vital path of communication. The administrative mechanism on which the President depended was again weakened.

The hostage dealings, in the meantime, fell into increasingly fewer hands. A crew-cut Marine Corps lieutenant colonel named Oliver North, in particular, took over control of the matter. North, an aide first to McFarlane and later to Poindexter, helped link the Iranian deals to an ill-fated operation: secret efforts to send arms and supplies to the Nicaraguan Contra rebels.

PROJECT DEMOCRACY

Reagan considered the Contras to be "freedom fighters" and railed against the leftist leaders of Nicaragua, charging them with spreading Communism in Central America. He wanted Congress to provide arms for the Contras, but Congress had its doubts, as did many Americans, about the often ineffective and unpopular rebel forces. Knowing the CIA was providing arms secretly to the Contras, in 1982 Congress passed the Boland Amendment, which limited and, in a later version, forbade most U.S. support of the rebels.

The National Security Council, however, secretly obtained funding for the Contras through channels outside of the federal government. In May 1984, McFarlane solicited help from foreign countries. Saudi Arabia was the first to contribute. Hoping for favors later, it gave the Contras one million dollars a month through secret bank accounts.

North and sometimes the CIA provided the Contras with military advice. And they organized the collection of funds from private donors, pouring millions of dollars into dummy corporations to buy arms, helicopters, and supplies for the Contras. These activities, dubbed "Project Democracy," were forbidden by the Boland Amendment, though the Reagan administration was later to dispute the constitutionality of this law.

In late 1985, North hiked the prices of arms being sold to Iran in exchange for hostages, realizing profits that were shifted to the Contras' Swiss bank accounts. It was clearly illegal — selling U.S. government property at a profit to finance a secret operation.

Reagan would later deny knowing about, much less authorizing, this activity. "They just didn't tell me what was going on," he said. North believed he did know. Poindexter, saying he was saving Reagan from responsibility, would first claim he never told the President about it. Later, Poindexter said Reagan did know.

A Retaliatory Air Strike

In the meantime, in April 1986, 10 days after a West German discotheque was bombed, killing a U.S. serviceman, the United States launched a retaliatory air raid on Libya. The North African nation was officially believed to be responsible for the disco bombing and other acts of anti-U.S. terrorism. Though many doubted that Libya was the main culprit in international terrorism, the attack was followed by a drop in terrorist acts. It rocketed Reagan to new heights of popularity.

UNRAVELING OF A SCANDAL

On October 5, 1986, a young Nicaraguan government soldier was on patrol when he looked up to the midday sky. To his astonishment, he saw a propeller-driven plane flying low overhead. He shouldered his tube anti-aircraft gun, aimed, and fired. The missile roared off and hit the camouflaged C-123 cargo plane, which exploded in flames and plummeted to the ground.

Eugene Hasenfus of Marinette, Wisconsin, was aboard the plane when it went down. He jumped out and floated to earth with a parachute, but he was captured by soldiers and paraded before reporters and their cameras. It soon became obvious, despite official denials, that he was part of a secret U.S. operation to supply the Contra rebels with arms.

This was one of a series of events and revelations that led to the exposure of the Iran-Contra affair.

Tarnished Presidency

Congress and the public were enraged. As the news media revealed details about what was going on, congressional investigations began to snowball. Despite efforts by North, Poindexter, and CIA chief William Casey to conceal their activities, by early 1987 sleuths would succeed in unearthing a paper and computer trail giving a detailed picture of the operations.

Reagan said nothing until mid-November, 1986, when he made his first public statement about the Iranian arms deal in a televised address. He seemed strained and defensive as he tried to explain away the flood of revelations:

> The charge has been made that the United States has shipped
> weapons to Iran as ransom payment for the release of American
> hostages in Lebanon; that the United States undercut its

allies and secretly violated American policy against trafficking with terrorists.

Those charges are utterly false. The United States has not made concessions to those who hold our people captive in Lebanon, and we will not. The United States has not swapped boatloads or planeloads of American weapons for the return of American hostages, and we will not.

Doubt Replaces Confidence

But this time the public did not respond to the Reagan touch in its usual way. Polls showed Americans believed that arms had been swapped for hostages and they opposed the trades. In one *Newsweek* poll, 90 percent of Americans said they did not believe Reagan was telling the truth about what he knew.

The President, who had won unprecedented confidence for his policies, was now being doubted. Only months before, on the Fourth of July, as he stood at the base of the Statue of Liberty for its 100th anniversary, he had been hailed by *Time* magazine as a "masterpiece of American magic." A headline called him "one of the strongest leaders of the 20th Century." By December, his overall approval rating, as measured by a *New York Times* poll, dropped from 67 to 46 percent in a single month. The 21-point drop was the largest one-month collapse ever recorded for any presidency.

Dealing with Failure

Reagan lashed out at the news media, blaming them for exposing the operations. He defended his staff, calling Lieutenant Colonel North, "a national hero." But soon he conceded in a radio address that "mistakes were made." It was the strongest admission of error Reagan would make.

The President believed he had done nothing wrong. Others disagreed. An aide said Nancy worried that Reagan might be impeached (brought to trial on charges of official wrongdoing). Some in Congress considered impeachment, but that body proved to have no stomach for such action so near the end of Reagan's last term.

In the face of this onslaught, Reagan withdrew for months into inactivity, unable to deal with his own failure. The White House came to a virtual standstill while the staff worked behind the scenes to reorganize. Sixteen months after *Time* magazine had so wildly hailed Reagan, it noted that "the nation calls for leadership and there is no one at home."

The Tower Commission

On February 26, 1987, an investigatory commission headed by Republican Senator John Tower and appointed by the White House itself presented a 304-page report. It said the arms sales would likely encourage elements in Iran to continue terrorist actions. It found the White House staff "doing what Congress forbade" in Nicaragua. Although Reagan told the commission he did not know the National Security Council was helping the Contra rebels, records show that he had been told about it many times.

The report blamed Reagan for his staff's activities. "He did not force his policy to undergo the most critical review . . . at no time did he insist upon accountability." He was depicted as a disengaged President who did not understand what was happening around him.

The Tower report blamed Chief of Staff Regan for "chaos" in the White House and for failing to keep the processes of administration orderly. After the report was released, Regan resigned. Nancy Reagan, who had never gotten along with Regan, waged a personal campaign in and out of the White House to encourage his departure.

Violation of Oath of Office

A separate *Select Committee Report* by congressional com-
mittees investigating the Iran-Contra affair said President Reagan had violated his oath of office. The majority concluded
in the report:

> The Constitution requires the President to 'take care that the
> law be faithfully executed.' This charge encompasses a respon-
> sibility to leave the members of his administration in no doubt
> that the rule of law governs. It was the President's policy—
> not an isolated decision by North or Poindexter—to sell arms
> secretly to Iran and maintain the Contras 'body and soul,' the
> Boland amendment notwithstanding. . . . For failing to care
> that the law reigned supreme, the President bears the
> responsibility.

The Iran-Contra affair would lead to criminal trials for
North, Poindexter, and a number of people in and outside
government. Reagan would leave office with many questions
still unanswered and deep suspicions about his involvement
in the Iran-Contra affair.

POWER SLIPS AWAY

Despite the adverse reports, Reagan's popularity hovered
around the 50 percent mark in the polls for the most of 1987
and 1988—not bad for a second-term President. By late 1988,
his approval rating had climbed to one of the highest of his
two terms. But Reagan's key policies were never as popular
as Reagan himself, and he lost more clout with Congress than
did most second-term Presidents. He never again enjoyed the
personal admiration that had been his as late as mid-1986.

At the end of 1987, Reagan's success rate with congressional legislation (the percentage of issues in which Congress supported his positions) fell to the lowest point for a President since the ratings were first compiled in 1953. This was due in part to losses in the 1986 congressional races that gave control of both the Senate and the House to the Democrats.

But it is doubtful that the Republicans would have lost so much in the election had Reagan's government not been so weakened. After 1986, Congress overrode presidential vetoes, rejected Reagan's Supreme Court nominations, and turned against the Contras. Congress had never before been so bold in its dealings with Reagan.

Abroad, the lack of presidential clout also was felt. Without continued backing, the Contras faded. In Panama, a drug-dealing dictator, Manuel Noriega, thumbed his nose at American attempts to oust him. In Lebanon, new hostage-takings pushed the number of captive Americans to nine, up from seven when the deals with Iran began. This suggested the arms-for-hostages efforts had encouraged terrorism.

Reagan, however, would find at least one bright spot in what seemed for him an unlikely place: Moscow's Red Square.

Chapter 12

To Moscow and Back

The road to Moscow began in front of the flickering warmth of a wood-burning fireplace in Geneva, Switzerland. There, in an elegant pool house attached to the official American villa, Reagan and Soviet leader Mikhail Gorbachev held their first summit meeting in November 1985. Accompanied only by their interpreters, they talked one-on-one about trust between nations, arms control, human rights, and regional conflicts. The 15 hours of friendly talks at the "fireside summit," reached no significant agreements and changed little except the mood of relations, but that was welcome.

ENDING THE COLD WAR

Reagan and Gorbachev agreed to meet again and to work for a 50 percent reduction in their arsenals of strategic weapons. Soon afterwards, in a show of goodwill, Soviet television broadcast an unedited five-minute speech by Reagan to the Soviet people. A similar speech by Gorbachev was broadcast in the United States. They met for a second time in Reykjavik, Iceland, late in 1986, but again came up with nothing. Talks snagged over Reagan's refusal to accept Soviet demands for an end to U.S. testing of "Star Wars" weapons.

But in 1987 the Soviets backed down, suggesting the United States and Soviet Union might destroy ground-based nuclear missiles without making this dependent on the United States stopping "Star Wars" testing. Negotiators went to work and by the end of the year came up with a deal. The agreement to destroy missiles, even though the weapons were to be of an unimportant type, made pioneering progress in reducing the threat of nuclear war.

On December 8, 1987, Reagan received Gorbachev at the White House and the leaders signed the Intermediate-range Nuclear Forces, or INF, Treaty, the first to require destruction of existing nuclear missiles.

Reagan went to Red Square in 1988 for his fourth summit with Gorbachev. The May 29-June 2 Moscow meeting reached no new agreements and was cooled by disagreements over human rights, but symbolically it became a watershed in U.S.-Soviet relations. The Cold War, many believed, was ending.

The breakthrough had much to do with the changes in the Soviet Union under Gorbachev and with the Soviet leader's diplomacy, but Reagan's government deserved some credit. His administration showed great flexibility and imagination. Reagan stood by his beliefs in the face of international pressure. He swung the support of U.S. conservatives behind an easing of Soviet–U.S. tensions as only another conservative like himself could do. No one would ever accuse Reagan of softness toward Moscow.

A Global Role for Defense

The willingness of Moscow to come to the conference table for arms talks was in part one of the results of the Reagan defense buildup. It put pressure on the Soviets, who were

On Moscow's Red Square, Soviet leader Mikhail Gorbachev holds a boy whom he had plucked from the arms of a passerby. The cozy scene, staged for the benefit of news cameras on May 31, 1988, seemed to represent Reagan's softer stance toward the Soviets. (Pete Souza, the White House.)

suffering their own economic difficulties, to reach agreements that would permit them to reduce defense spending.

The U.S. military resurgence ironed out many post-Vietnam War defense problems. Training was upgraded, strategic forces received a needed boost, and morale in the military rose to new heights. The armed forces at the end of Reagan's presidency were considered by many to be the best in U.S. peacetime history.

The new military strength helped America reassert itself overseas in a way it had not done since the Vietnam War. Reagan used U.S. military might to send naval escorts to the Persian Gulf to protect ships from the spreading Iran-Iraq war. Though there was loss of life when ships came under attack and a U.S. warship accidentally shot down an Iranian passenger airliner, the maneuver demonstrated U.S. readiness to defend the free flow of oil and stand up to threats of intimidation. The legacy of timidity left by the Vietnam War seemed to have been overcome.

Improved military readiness, however, cost U.S. taxpayers $2.5 trillion over the eight years of Reagan's presidency, with a portion of that lost to waste and overspending. The government was spending 35 percent above 1980 levels on defense by the end of Reagan's second term. This became an expense the United States could hardly afford.

DOMESTIC LEGACIES

In his last creative act in domestic legislation, Reagan presided over a reform of tax laws in 1986. The tax-reform package, building on first-term measures, lowered the top tax rate from 70 percent to 28 percent. It also removed thousands of taxpayers at the lower end of the income scale from the tax rolls. The tax reforms accelerated economic growth and inspired a worldwide move away from high taxes designed to redistribute wealth.

The bigger economic picture looked bright in Reagan's second term. Inflation remained under control, sliding from 12 percent in 1980 to 4.4 percent in 1988. Unemployment in that same year hit a 14-year low of 5.3 percent. Economic expansion following the 1981–1982 recession continued for the remaining seven years of the Reagan presidency.

Looming over all this, however, fears over the economy's future shadowed Reagan's last years. On "Black Monday," October 19, 1987, the stock market suffered a catastrophic collapse. Although it recovered its former peaks within two years, the sudden steep decline jarred the foundations of finance.

The Growing National Debt

An emphasis on government deregulation of business during the Reagan years discouraged careful scrutiny of savings and loan institutions and led to widespread, costly failures. Wall Street engaged in sometimes wasteful takeovers of businesses, while the stagnation of basic research for civilian uses enabled foreign companies to gain a competitive edge over American industry. The greatest economic concern, however, surrounded the budget deficit, which averaged $180 billion during 1982–1988.

To cover the growing difference, the Reagan administration went into debt, which, in 1988, stood at a record $2.6 trillion. In 1980, when Reagan was elected, the government owed $914 billion, and it cost $71 billion a year to pay off the U.S. debt. By 1988, it was costing $152 billion a year to pay the national debt, sopping up badly needed funds. In that year, the interest on the debt exceeded the budgets of nine federal departments—Agriculture, Commerce, Education, Energy, Interior, Justice, Labor, State, and Transportation. The cost of the debt was expected to take many years to pay off.

In the long term, the national debt was seen as weakening future U.S. economic vitality and sapping trading power in the international economy. Instead of being a lending nation, in control of its funds, the country became the world's leading debtor, owing more money than any other nation on Earth. And it had to sacrifice a measure of independence as it accepted money from banks in Japan, Saudi Arabia, and other industrial nations in order to balance its books. Commentators considered the high national deficit to be Reagan's greatest policy failure.

The Shape of Society

Reagan came to the presidency with dreams of reversing nearly 50 years of welfare state programs dating back to Franklin Delano Roosevelt. He wanted to give free enterprise and individual responsibility a greater role in American society. But after two terms, most of the social, health, and housing services he aimed to reduce were still intact, although weakened, by cuts totaling $45 billion. The number of federal employees, however, increased by tens of thousands — mostly in the defense area.

State governments managed to get by, increasing their own activities or taxes to make up for decreased help from the federal government. Efforts by states to attract foreign investment rose nationwide. A national decline in the quality of education was met at the state level, as more than 40 states passed laws calling for educational improvements. In certain areas, less federal involvement forced local people to become more self-reliant. The Reagan policies encouraged voluntary work and giving to charity.

But an array of social problems grew worse during the Reagan years. Blame for this situation was laid in part on the cutbacks in federal spending. These reductions contributed to growing problems of homelessness and funding shortfalls in higher education. Availability of medical care for the poor and elderly declined as government medical programs shrank. By the end of Reagan's second term, use of illegal drugs, illiteracy, and crime had all increased. The elderly had become more affluent, but one-fifth of America's children lived in poverty.

A Move to the Right

One of Reagan's lasting actions was the appointment of conservatives to the federal courts, especially the Supreme Court. These judges serve for life terms, making interpretations of the law that affect all aspects of society. For the first time in a generation, Reagan's three appointments to the Supreme Court put conservatives in a 5 to 4 majority that was expected to last long after he left office.

Reagan's appointees to the Supreme Court included the first woman Justice, Sandra Day O'Connor. They overturned precedents and made conservative judgments on issues that included abortion and racial and sexual discrimination. A conservative social agenda that Reagan was unable to carry out through congressional legislation, such as measures to limit abortion and restrict affirmative action hiring plans, was advanced under Supreme Court decisions.

Many of these decisions triggered an uproar from the country's liberals, but by the end of his administration, they were fighting an uphill battle. Reagan changed the political landscape of America. Not only the courts, but the entire spectrum of debate shifted to the right, bringing Reagan's brand of conservatism from the fringes into the mainstream of the American political structure.

ALL ROADS LEAD TO DIXON

By late summer of 1988, attention had shifted away from the Reagan administration to the presidential election campaigns. Reagan stayed in the background until it appeared that Vice-President George Bush would win the Republican presidential nomination. The President's endorsement, when it came, appeared late and lukewarm.

Even so, a good deal of the Reagan magic rubbed off on the less charismatic Bush. At the Republican National Convention in August, delegates would cheer wildly when Reagan mounted the stage. After Labor Day, Reagan campaigned effectively in a race that turned into a bitter mud-slinging match between Bush and his Democratic opponent, Massachusetts Governor Michael Dukakis. Bush won handily, but with margins far short of Reagan's victories.

Welcome to California

The tourists gawked at the tall iron gate at 668 St. Cloud Drive in exclusive Bel-Air, California, a part of Hollywood. There wasn't much to look at, just the gate. High stone walls studded with detection devices fanned out in both directions from the gate. But this was not just another Hollywood movie star's hideaway.

This one was the retirement home of Nancy and Ronald Reagan. The house, purchased by 18 friends for $2.5 million and leased to the Reagans for $15,000 a month, overlooked Los Angeles. Equipped with servants' quarters, a swimming pool, and a greenhouse, the 7,000-square-foot, ranch-style home was marked only by the street number 668, which was changed from the original 666 when the new occupants moved in. Nancy Reagan, being superstitious, had it changed because "666" in the New Testament Book of Revelation is associated with Satan. Old habits die hard.

The Unretiring Reagans

After the January 20, 1989, inauguration of George Bush as the 41st President of the United States, Reagan left office with the usual rounds of advice-giving, farewells, and a symbolic exchange of salutes with his successor. He and Nancy settled into the new house in California, where they are leading relatively private lives. On Sundays they attend the local Bel-Air Presbyterian Church.

On weekdays, Reagan makes a 20-minute commute to a downtown suite of offices set up to handle his affairs. Nancy has offices in the same building for her Nancy Reagan Foundation to fight drug abuse. At the office, Reagan works on his presidential memoirs, answers mail, and reviews the flood of requests to give speeches, interviews, or make appearances. He turns many down, but once in a while, he gives a speech and reminisces about old times.

"The White House was very pleasant, you know," Reagan told an enthusiastic crowd of 4,000 Young Republicans at Pepperdine University shortly after leaving office. "It was just wonderful there. But a Californian, away for eight years, lives in a little state of homesickness." The students at the Malibu, California, institution understood. They gave the former President a souvenir surfboard.

GOING HOME AGAIN

One Sunday in 1989, a flight instructor in a small plane high over Illinois heard the voice of a pilot make a radio call to the air traffic controller. "We'd like to be cleared to 12,000 feet over Dixon," said the pilot of a private jet. "We have President Reagan on board, and he'd like to take a look at his hometown." The controller was heard to consent, and the plane swooped down over Dixon.

For five or six minutes the plane circled as the former President, who was passing over Illinois on the return trip from a Chicago speaking engagement, happily commented on the sites below for everyone on board. Reagan told stories and recalled memories of the city of his boyhood as the plane flew low to enable the passengers to see distinctly the buildings of the town of 15,710 people.

"President Reagan was clearly enjoying himself, so we kept circling," said aide Mark Weinberg. "I got the impression that circling over Dixon and looking down at those buildings was a highlight of the trip for him. It was a special thing. Everything he could see on the ground would prompt him to reminisce. He was sharing his memories with us."

The local flight instructor, who overheard the call from the private jet's pilot, later learned of what had come to pass through a newspaper columnist who tracked down the details of the incident. "This is sort of amazing," said the flight instructor. "People come to our airfield all the time to charter little planes so they can look at their homes from the air. And here's Ronald Reagan, doing the same thing.

"Come to think of it, though, it's not so amazing at all. It almost makes sense."

Bibliography

Cannon, Lou. *Reagan*. New York: G. P. Putman's Sons, 1982. An in-depth biography covering the California years and early presidency.

Edwards, Anne. *Early Reagan*. New York: William Morrow, 1987. A thorough and detailed history of Reagan's childhood, education, and career up to 1965.

Friedman, Stanley P. *Ronald Reagan: His Life Story in Pictures*. New York: Dodd, Mead, 1986. An array of well-selected pictures with brief biographical text.

Germond, Jack W., and Witcover, Jules. *Wake Us When It's Over: Presidential Politics of 1984*. New York: MacMillan, 1985. A detailed history of the 1984 presidential election campaign.

Harwood, Richard, editor. *The Pursuit of the Presidency 1980*. New York: G.P. Putman's Sons, 1980. A compilation of reports by the *Washington Post* on the 1980 campaign for the presidency.

Hertsgaard, Mark. *On Bended Knee*. New York: Farrar Straus Giroux, 1988. A careful analysis of the news media coverage of the Reagan presidency.

Mayer, Jane, and McManus, Doyle. *Landslide: The Unmaking of the President: 1984–1988*. Boston: Houghton Mifflin, 1988. An excellent and readable account of the Iran-Contra affair.

Reagan, Ronald, and Hubler, Richard G. *Where's the Rest of Me?* New York: Dell, 1965. Reagan's autobiography written in 1964 in preparation for his political career.

Smith, Elizabeth Simpson. *Five First Ladies: A Look into the Lives of Nancy Reagan, Rosalynn Carter, Betty Ford, Pat Nixon, and Lady Bird Johnson.* New York: Walker and Company, 1986. A young readers' book including a well-written biographical sketch of Nancy Reagan.

Stockman, David A. *The Triumph of Politics: How the Reagan Revolution Failed.* New York: Harper and Row, 1986. The well-reported and substantial story of Reaganomics as told by Reagan's first-term budget director.

Thomas, Tony. *The Films of Ronald Reagan.* Secaucus, NJ: Citadel Press, 1980. A more detailed history of Reagan's film career.

Wills, Garry. *Reagan's America.* Garden City, NY: Doubleday, 1987. A rich biography describing the historical and cultural roots of Reagan's ideas.

Index

Iran-Iraq war, 113
Iranian hostage crisis, 74–75, 76, 83,
    99–100, 101

Johnson, Ellen Marie, and "The
    Johnson Professional Players,"
    17, 31
Johnson, Lyndon B., 58, 83

Kennedy, John F., 54, 55
"Kings Row" (film), 37
"Knute Rockne-All American"
    (film), 35
Ku Klux Klan, 11, 74

Lebanon, 82, 83, 98, 101, 109
Libya, 104

MacArthur, Peter, 23–24
Marines, U.S., 82
McFarlane, Robert "Bud," 98,
    101–102, 103
McKinzie, Ralph, 12, 19
Meese, Edwin, 62, 87
Middle East, 81 82
Mondale, Walter F., 94
Moscow, Soviet Union, 1, 2, 109, 111
Music Corporation of America
    (MCA), 52, 53, 55, 64

Nancy Reagan Foundation, 118
National Security Council, 91, 97,
    101, 103, 107
New Deal, 22, 24, 28, 29–30, 55
New Right, 55
Newsweek (magazine), 83, 84, 106
Nicaragua, 82, 107
Nixon, Richard, 54, 63, 67, 83
Nofziger, Lyn, 60, 61
Noriega, Manuel, 109
North Dixon High School, 10, 12
North, Oliver, 103, 104, 106, 108
Notre Dame University, 35

O'Connor, Sandra Day, 116

Panama, 109
Panama Canal, 69
Parsons, Luella, 37
Pearl Harbor, Hawaii, 39
Poindexter, John M., 102, 103, 104, 108

Rancho Del Cielo, California, 64
Reagan, Jack (father of Ronald Rea-
    gan), 3, 4, 5, 7, 9, 10–11, 19–20,
    24, 25, 27, 33, 35–37
Reagan, John Neil "Moon" (brother
    of Ronald Reagan), 4, 5, 7, 11,
    19, 24, 25, 28, 38–39, 43
Reagan, Maureen (daughter of
    Ronald Reagan), 38, 47
Reagan, Michael (son of Ronald
    Reagan), 47
Reagan, Nancy Davis (second wife
    of Ronald Reagan), 50 52, 54,
    64–65, 71, 72, 75, 88–91, 103,
    107, 117, 118
Reagan, Nelle (mother of Ronald
    Reagan), 3, 4, 5, 7, 8, 11, 14,
    19, 25, 27, 33, 55
Reagan, Patricia Ann "Patti" (daugh-
    ter of Ronald Reagan), 54
Reagan, Ronald Prescott "Skipper"
    (son of Ronald Reagan), 54
Reagan, Ronald W.,
    acting career of, 30–32, 34–38, 49
    in the Air Force, 39–40
    assassination attempt on, 77–78
    boyhood of, 3–11
    Cabinet of, 87–88
    campaign of for governor of
        California, 1967, 58–59
    campaign of for President, 1980,
        70–75
    campaign of for President, 1984,
        93–96

124   *Ronald W. Reagan*

presidential nomination, 1968,
63, 68–72
as a Democrat, 39, 40, 54, 55
education of, 7, 8, 10, 12–20
as a football player, 12, 13, 16, 17–18
as governor of California, 60–66
management style of, 62–63, 64,
86, 98, 100–101
marriage of to Jane Wyman,
33–34, 47–49
marriage of to Nancy Davis, 52
nicknames of, 5, 35, 84, 85
presidency of, 75–116
radio career of, 23–28, 30
religion of, 7, 118
as a Republican, 55, 56–58
retirement of, 117–119
and the Screen Actors Guild
(SAG), 44–45, 46, 52–53
Supreme Court nominations by,
109, 116
television career of, 53–55
"Reaganomics," 80
Recession, of 1982, 79–80, 93, 114
"Red-baiting," 44, 45, 50, 54
"Red menace," 43; *see also* Communism
Regan, Donald, 86, 89, 101, 103, 107
Republican National Conventions,
63, 69, 117
Republicans, 39, 45, 54, 55, 56–57,
67–68, 96, 109, 118
Robbins, Anne Frances, *see* Reagan,
Nancy Davis
Roberts, Bill, 58, 59
Rockne, Knute, 35
Roosevelt, Franklin Delano, 22, 23,
24, 25, 28, 39, 40, 55, 56, 94, 115

Schary, Dore and Miriam, 50, 51
Schultz, George, 87, 98, 100, 102
Screen Actors Guild (SAG), 44, 45,
46, 51, 52–53

Sears, John, 68, 70, 71
Select Committee Report, 108
Soviet Union, 1, 2, 81, 110–111
Speech," "The, 53, 55, 57, 68
Spencer, Stuart, 58, 59, 68
"Stallion Road" (film), 47
"Star Wars," 81, 111
Stockman, David, 79, 80, 93, 98
Strategic Defense Initiative, 81
Supply-side economics, 69, 70, 78,
79, 80
Supreme Court, U.S., 116

Tampico, Illinois, 3, 4, 7, 8
Taxes, 59, 62–63, 66, 68, 70, 75, 78,
79, 80, 93, 113
Television, 53–55, 57–58, 61, 71, 73,
74, 84–85, 95–96, 110
Terrorism, 99, 104, 109
"This Is the Army" (film), 40
Time (magazine), 106, 107
Tower, John, 107
Truman, Harry, 40, 81
TWA flight 847, hijacking of, 97–98,
99–100, 101
20th Century Fox, 64

Vietnam War, 74, 83, 113

Warner Brothers studios, 31, 43, 47, 49
Watergate affair, 67
Watt, James G., 88
Weinberger, Casper, 100, 102
WHO, radio station in Des Moines,
Iowa, 25, 26, 31
Where's the Rest of Me? (Reagan au-
tobiography), 38, 55
WOC, radio station in Davenport,
Iowa, 23–24, 25
World War II, 39, 40
Wyman, Jane (first wife of Ronald
Reagan), 33–34, 35, 38, 45,
47–49

PRESIDENTS OF THE UNITED STATES

GEORGE WASHINGTON	L. Falkof	0-944483-19-4
JOHN ADAMS	R. Stefoff	0-944483-10-0
THOMAS JEFFERSON	R. Stefoff	0-944483-07-0
JAMES MADISON	B. Polikoff	0-944483-22-4
JAMES MONROE	R. Stefoff	0-944483-11-9
JOHN QUINCY ADAMS	M. Greenblatt	0-944483-21-6
ANDREW JACKSON	R. Stefoff	0-944483-08-9
MARTIN VAN BUREN	R. Ellis	0-944483-12-7
WILLIAM HENRY HARRISON	R. Stefoff	0-944483-54-2
JOHN TYLER	L. Falkof	0-944483-60-7
JAMES K. POLK	M. Greenblatt	0-944483-04-6
ZACHARY TAYLOR	D. Collins	0-944483-17-8
MILLARD FILLMORE	K. Law	0-944483-61-5
FRANKLIN PIERCE	F. Brown	0-944483-25-9
JAMES BUCHANAN	D. Collins	0-944483-62-3
ABRAHAM LINCOLN	R. Stefoff	0-944483-14-3
ANDREW JOHNSON	R. Stevens	0-944483-16-X
ULYSSES S. GRANT	L. Falkof	0-944483-02-X
RUTHERFORD B. HAYES	N. Robbins	0-944483-23-2
JAMES A. GARFIELD	F. Brown	0-944483-63-1
CHESTER A. ARTHUR	R. Stevens	0-944483-05-4
GROVER CLEVELAND	D. Collins	0-944483-01-1
BENJAMIN HARRISON	R. Stevens	0-944483-15-1
WILLIAM McKINLEY	D. Collins	0-944483-55-0
THEODORE ROOSEVELT	R. Stefoff	0-944483-09-7
WILLIAM H. TAFT	L. Falkof	0-944483-56-9
WOODROW WILSON	D. Collins	0-944483-18-6
WARREN G. HARDING	A. Canadeo	0-944483-64-X
CALVIN COOLIDGE	R. Stevens	0-944483-57-7

HERBERT C. HOOVER	B. Polikoff	0-944483-58-5
FRANKLIN D. ROOSEVELT	M. Greenblatt	0-944483-06-2
HARRY S. TRUMAN	D. Collins	0-944483-00-3
DWIGHT D. EISENHOWER	R. Ellis	0-944483-13-5
JOHN F. KENNEDY	L. Falkof	0-944483-03-8
LYNDON B. JOHNSON	L. Falkof	0-944483-20-8
RICHARD M. NIXON	R. Stefoff	0-944483-59-3
GERALD R. FORD	D. Collins	0-944483-65-8
JAMES E. CARTER	D. Richman	0-944483-24-0
RONALD W. REAGAN	N. Robbins	0-944483-66-6
GEORGE H.W. BUSH	R. Stefoff	0-944483-67-4

GARRETT EDUCATIONAL CORPORATION
130 EAST 13TH STREET
ADA, OK 74820